SLANT

WRITING ESSAYS YOU WANT TO READ

Second Edition

Nicholas Leither
& Barry Horwitz

Second Edition

ISBN-13:
978-0997808605

ISBN-10:
0997808608

For more information and teaching tools:

www.NicholasLeither.com

CONTENTS

About this Book
To Students and Instructors

The Idea

The idea at the core of this writing textbook is that every essay writing class is a creative writing class. One of the unfortunate malfunctions of teaching essay writing has been its separation from creative writing, which often seems like more fun to students.

However, everyone who has ever been in a rigorous creative writing class knows that poetry, fiction, and memoir have all the same elements and expectations that essay writing classes do. A creative writer must include structure, style and compelling content. The differences between the two have to do merely with purpose, not with creation or discipline.

On the one hand, students often like the appeal of creative writing because they believe there are fewer rules. They often rightly believe that in a creative writing class they can more accurately "be themselves" in their writing, have more fun, and express their ideas in a less constrained form—one that encourages their own "voice." When they write academic essays, they frequently feel they have to write in a dull, boring, and monotone voice. They often believe they are supposed to be learning how to write like someone else. That's tragic.

Slant's purpose is to help correct that. However, I didn't write *Slant* to support this idea that writing is a free-for-all or that it doesn't have rigorous expectations. If a student takes a class called "The Fundamentals of Drawing," the teacher isn't going to just stick a sheet of paper in front of the student with some pencils and say, "Art is like totally free, so just draw whatever." She would set up a vase next to some fruit and an empty bottle and ask the student to draw the still life. She would teach the line, shading, shadowing and perspective. Being an artist takes training. And let's be honest, it's not always as easy and pleasurable as we sometimes hope it might be. However, that doesn't mean that it has to be dull, formulaic, or completely devoid of the writer's voice and personal style.

Writing instruction currently suffers from two core malfunctions: Making simple teachings too difficult, and making difficult teachings artless and too simple. When we teach writing, there are things that are relatively easy to teach and things that are almost impossible to teach. You can teach a student how to structure a paragraph, for example, but teaching him or her how to develop an engaging and personal writing voice in that paragraph is like trying to meditate in Times Square. We often spend too much time trying to teach students how to "style" an essay—too much time trying to control and limit their writing tone, their personal voices, their formality and informality—instead of encouraging them to practice, experiment, and take stylistic and creative risks. Because of our desire for our students' success, we sometimes forget that teaching structure is a catalyst for both critical thinking *and* the development of a writer's creative and personal style.

I wrote *Slant* because I wanted to teach students how to structure their own ideas in an essay in order for them to engage actively and creatively in the process of writing. The best advice I ever got about writing was from a writing professor in college named Stacy Pies. In the hallway after class I asked her if I could write my essay in the style of an investigate newspaper journalist. She shrugged.

"Try it."

The Creation

I first learned how to teach writing from my graduate school teacher, mentor and colleague, Barry Horwitz, who taught writing for over thirty years at the Sorbonne in Paris, the University of California, Berkeley, and Saint Mary's College of California. After I graduated with an MFA in writing, I began teaching composition. Barry and I collaborated for years on our method of teaching writing. We discussed it often, co-taught writing courses, reviewed many writing and rhetoric textbooks, created writing projects across the curriculum, and conferred extensively about teaching.

 After I completed the first draft of *Slant*, I offered it to the college community free of charge for three years in proof form. Over forty instructors used *Slant*. Many of them discussed it with me, offered their criticism, and made suggestions. Over those three years, I revised *Slant* continually based on my own teaching, and the criticism I received from other instructors, students, and Barry Horwitz.

Now in its second edition, this book has gone through an intensive and collaborative review process. Most textbooks are peer reviewed by other instructors who read the texts and provide feedback, but *Slant's* review process was and continues to be unique. Instead of instructors simply reading *Slant*, they used it in their classrooms and we worked together to improve it. This revised textbook has had over five years of classroom testing, and I am very thankful and indebted to the instructors who worked with and supported me, especially Rosa del Duca, Victoria Phillips, Elise Miller, Naomi Schwartz, Charlie Hamaker, Frances Sweeney, Maura Tarnoff, and Stefanie Silva.

Readers should understand that *Slant* is not reinventing the wheel. *Slant* compiles the working methods and ideas I have found in my own teaching of writing, in other instructors' use of *Slant*, and in my research and experimentation with writing textbooks. I have attempted to simplify the aspects of writing instruction I have found overly complicated, and eliminate ineffective and unnecessary methods.

Many people say that there are two types of writers: painters and sculptors. Painters keep adding layers and sculptors carve pieces away. In creating *Slant* I did both. I kept adding layers, and removing the excess. What follows is a step-by-step guide through the creative process of writing an academic essay.

Comments Welcome

Please do not hesitate to contact me with your questions or suggestions for *Slant*. Writing instruction is a pliant and always-changing thing, and I by no means claim to hold the "truths" or suggest that *Slant* is perfect. Both student and instructor feedback is welcome. It's what made *Slant* successful from the beginning. Tell me how *Slant* works for you.

Website

For contact information, and further information about *Slant*, including downloads, assignments, sample essay projects, and the Crescendo Analysis Labs, please visit my website:

www.NicholasLeither.com

Barry Horwitz and Nicholas Leither in the Sahara

Author's Note: Attention Writers!

What do you do when your instructor assigns an essay? Do you sigh? Do you think about murder? Do you crack another Redbull, pop on your headphones, and hope you don't fall asleep on your keyboard? Do you wonder why it isn't more fun?

Well, it's partly your fault. I'm serious. If writing is a pain in the neck, then you're trying too hard to make it a pain in the neck. You're the one who holds the cards here. It's time to start owning it.

That's *Slant*, in a nutshell. *Slant* is about you following your interests, engaging your curiosity, using your own voice and creativity, and writing like a reader. It's not just about writing A essays, but about writing great essays and enjoying the process.

This book doesn't teach you how to write. Really, you already know how to do that. Instead, it puts you where you belong as a writer—in the control seat. Here, you will find fundamental and creative suggestions and examples that will stimulate your curiosity, help you develop your ideas, and lead you to phenomenal writing.

<<<>>>

When I was an undergraduate at New York University, I took an American Literature class. We were reading *Tender is the Night* by F. Scott Fitzgerald, and I was in my professor's office, ranting to her about all the critical essays I had just skimmed about the novel and the ideas I had come across. She stopped me and said, "All good, but what do *you* think?"

I fell silent, then mumbled something that obviously didn't impress her because she said, "Look, you're an American, right? You're a reader. You've read everything Fitzgerald ever wrote, and you've read a lot of American literature. You can have an opinion."

I probably argued. I probably told her that yes, I'm an American, and yes, I've read everything Fitzgerald wrote, but I wasn't alive during the Jazz Age.

But, she had a point. I realized that college, and especially writing, isn't just about gathering other people's opinions, but about presenting your own *Slant*.

-Nicholas Leither

How to Use this Book

What the Heck is *Slant*?

Simple definition: Your opinion. Complicated definition: Your ideas, the way you communicate in writing, your perspective and point of view, even your thesis. Your *Slant* is anything and everything that makes your essay you. Because your thesis is your purpose and your opinion, the core of your *Slant* is your thesis. But because it takes more than a thesis to make an argument, *Slant* extends far beyond the thesis into the way you express yourself in writing.

Many of you have probably read a piece of writing that was full of facts and support and evidence for its argument. However, the essay was so dull and poorly structured that when you reached the end you didn't feel like you trusted the writer. You also have probably read an essay that was short on facts, evidence and support, but was written so stylishly, with such a conversational and engaging style that by the time you reached the end you trusted and wanted to believe the writer. That's an important lesson, and it defines the word *Slant*. While strong support and evidence are crucial in writing an engaging and persuasive essay, the way you express yourself as a writer, the way you structure your sentences and paragraphs, have a strong impact on readers.

For a moment, think of your essay like a song. The core of the *Slant* is in the lyrics, right? But lyrics alone don't make a song. You've got the singer and the way she sings it. You've got instruments and rhythm and a chorus. And if you bring all of these different parts together to make the lyrics really sing, you've got a masterpiece. When you go beyond writing an essay you have to write and actually write an essay you would want to read, every sentence and paragraph will have your ideas, your voice, and your *Slant*.

Student Writer: Jennifer Tang

Jennifer Tang was an English major at Saint Mary's College of California, where she wrote two essays which we're going to use throughout *Slant* as examples. The first essay, "Being Innately Woman," Jennifer explores the rebellious roles of Clytaemenstra in the play "Agamemnon" by Aeschylus, and Antigone in the play "Antigone" by Sophocles. Her second essay, "Picking up the Heavy Nozzle—Scary, Right?" explores the cultural implications of the American gas station.

Student Writer: Lydia Davidson

Lydia Davidson was a music major at Santa Clara University when she wrote "Quitting Cold Turkey." After reading Jonathan Safran Foer's *Eating Animals* and David Foster Wallace's essay "Consider the Lobster," Lydia realized the importance of detail, specificity, and her own qualifications as a writer. Stirred to change her own eating habits because of what she learned, she wrote an essay about the American holiday of Thanksgiving, which allowed her to unpack the tense and sticky issues of education, ethics, habit, and provocation in the context of her own family's holiday.

Student Writer: Pablo Rocha

Portions of Pablo Rocha's essay project about F. Scott Fitzgerald's *The Great Gatsby* appear here, called "A Father's Advice."

The Structure of Each Chapter: The ARC
Approach, Rehearse, Create

The idea of an "arc"—whether in an essay, a book, or even architecture—begins in one place, changes, and ends in a new place. The same idea applies here in *Slant*. Each chapter in this book is broken up into three sections. Like the whole of *Slant*, each chapter demonstrates a step-by-step process.

The first section of each chapter, **Approach**, introduces the ideas of the exercises and writing that continue in Rehearse and Create.

The second section, **Rehearse**, is composed of methods and pre-writing exercises that prepare you for composition.

The third section, **Create**, guides you through the writing process of a particular part of the essay. This is the core of every chapter—the point at which you're ready to start creating.

Don't Put *Slant* Down
Step by Step Writing

If you approach an essay like it's merely an obligation, it's going to read like an obligation. However, if you think of your essay like it's an adventurous trip into the unknown, it will read like one. Think of *Slant* like it's a guidebook—a tattered volume that contains all the information you need about the sights you're about to see, the food you might eat, and the places you might sleep. It's a guidebook you're going to need to refer to at every stage of your adventure. But it doesn't create the adventure for you. Only you can do that.

Don't put it down. Like traveling, there are times when you feel like you can manage on your own, only to find that you're lost and sick in some place without a telephone. Stick to *Slant*. Trust *Slant*. Writing is a process, and working through this book guides you through that process. If your essay is Mount Everest, *Slant* is your *Sherpa*.

What SLANT Doesn't Do

Slant can guide you through the creative writing and structuring of an essay. However, it doesn't teach you how to create an MLA works cited page. It doesn't teach you how to research a topic. It doesn't teach you sentence structure or grammar. Instead, *Slant*, carries you through the process of creating a topic, writing a thesis, forming an outline, drafting your essay, and revising your essay.

Developing the Way You Write

Slant is not going to teach you some drastically foreign process of writing an essay. It's not going to undermine what many of you have learned in previous writing classes. For example, if you're under the impression that a thesis statement should be the first sentence of your essay or that the first paragraph needs to be an "introduction," you're going to learn how to develop that into a more successful and intricate structure. You are now ready to take writing to the next level.

If you learned somewhere that a thesis appears in your essay as one sentence, get ready to spread it out.

If you're under the impression that you must repeat your thesis in your conclusion, prepare to modify.

Every essay needs to have a logical structure, but essays don't just follow a "formula." If you've been writing five-paragraph essays, *Slant* is going to help you take that structure and build it into something bigger and better—a stylish, more sophisticated essay.

Slant isn't about dropping everything you've ever done and changing it all. It's about building it up into writing you would want to read.

But I Have to Write a "Literary Analysis" Essay

An essay is an essay. Sure, there are different types of essays and every essay has its own "idea" and road to travel. But no matter what kind of essay you're trying to write, be it literary analysis, comparison and contrast, research, or even personal, every essay has an argument and a logical structure. Every essay has a *Slant*.

For the purposes of *Slant*, the word "support" signifies both the use of the text in a literary analysis essay and the use of primary and secondary evidence in a research essay.

You are the Artist. Follow the Fear.

What often makes a masterpiece is a sense of risk and adventure and creativity in the writing. Sometimes students tell me that the reason they choose broad topics is because they seem easy to support. If you want to fail before you begin, make easiness your main concern. When a writer challenges him- or herself, a great essay often results. You will **never** write a great essay if you don't follow the fear.

1: Creating a Topic

Approach

1. Chasing Excitement

Boring. We've all felt that way when facing an essay. But most of us have felt thrilled writing essays too. And the reason we felt thrilled is because we were excited and interested in the topic.

That's why choosing a topic and developing a thesis is such an important step in the writing process. It's your chance to choose a focus that thrills you. The worst thing to write about is something you think *sounds* good, or something you think your teacher wants. If you choose a topic that excites you, one that stimulates your mind and provokes questions, your essay is going to read wonderfully, and every step of the writing process will be full of new discoveries.

Too many students believe that an assignment is some kind of formula they need to fill in for the instructor. Wrong. Assignments merely present guidelines to help you get going. Time to take those lemons and make lemonade.

Follow your interest. If you're writing about a text, re-read the sentences and paragraphs you've marked or noted. If you're writing a research essay, do some preliminary research. Trust yourself as a reader. When you find yourself questioning an idea, it's probably because you're curious about it. Develop it. And let's repeat this so it becomes a mantra: *Follow your interest. Follow your interest.*

2. Exploring the Unknown

After you've discovered a question or topic that interests you, it's time for some easy development. Take some notes. Try some free-writing. Do some reading and research. Sit at your desk or in the library or at a café with a magazine or a notebook and contemplate the topic.

Spend ten minutes thinking about that topic. After ten minutes is up, forget everything that came to mind and start from where you left off. Remember, in that first ten minutes, everything you think about is "the known." It's what everyone else is going to think about too. After ten minutes of contemplation, you're ready to start developing a thesis and exploring "the unknown."

Don't jump right in. Be patient. The more preparation you do here, the easier it's going to be later in the writing process. One of the biggest mistakes students often make in this early stage is thinking that an idea is just going to magically come to them, and if it doesn't there's nothing he or she can do. Creating a topic is active, not passive. A topic doesn't just arrive; you have to seek it out. You have to investigate. The exercises in the Rehearse section will help you do just that.

3. Collaboration

One of the best ways to develop or discover a topic is to elicit ideas from others. You do it all the time. Perhaps you're sitting in your room, talking with your friends and you say, "Why do you think gas prices are so erratic?" It's a vague question. It's meant only to stimulate discussion about a topic in which you're interested. But it works wonders. Those conversations can lead to deep and specific ideas and issues.

There are many ways to collaborate. A simple discussion with friends is a great start. A written survey is another idea. A question in a class discussion focused on your topic will provoke informed answers from your peers. Try calling your mom. Even better, meet with your instructor. Why do it all alone? Get others involved.

4. Following the Fear: Narrowing

About 98.7 percent of the essays I read in composition courses are too broad. I like to say that it's almost impossible to have a thesis that's too narrow. If you're reading Homer's *Odyssey* and you ask a question like, "Is Odysseus a hero?" the answers could cover volumes. A narrower question might be, "Is Odysseus the hero of the *Odyssey*?" That question, though still too broad for a short essay, focuses on the text and leads you to compare Odysseus to other characters and their heroic actions. "Does Odysseus's breach of integrity when he spends the year romantically involved with Circe damage his honorable reputation?" In this question we've moved past the vague implications of the word "hero" and questioned Odysseus's integrity and honor. A thesis based on this topic question may be narrow enough for a five to ten page essay.

 A broader topic *seems* easier at first because you could probably open Homer's *Odyssey* up to a random page and find support for Odysseus being a hero. However, you're never going to be able to properly prove and support such a vague claim in a short essay. Follow the fear to a narrow and specific topic. Throughout *Slant*, you will see how Jennifer, Pablo, and Lydia all narrowed and specified their ideas and essays.

Rehearse

Look over the six exercises and pick one or two to complete.

1. Starting with a Question
If you ask a question, the thesis—or Slant—of your essay is the answer.

It's a pretty simple idea. If you ask a question, chances are you're curious about the answer. Right there is a great reason to develop that topic. Remember, you don't have to know the answer. It's the writing and development process that will lead you to your own answer. It's okay to remain neutral, especially at first.

Think of the writing process as a science experiment. You start with a question, or what's called a hypothesis. You then test that hypothesis with experiments. After the test, you write a conclusion about your findings. Well, that's just like an essay. Ask a question. Formulate an answer. Test that thesis by writing, researching and referring to the text. And write a conclusion.

If you ask a question, the thesis or *Slant* of your essay is the answer. After Jennifer read the book *Oil on the Brain* by Lisa Margonelli, she had a few questions about gas stations:

1.	Why is there so much violence at gas stations?
2.	Why do cop shows often focus on gas station crime?
3.	Why are gas stations dangerous?
4.	How did the American gas station become a headquarters for fear?

After mulling over these questions, Jennifer came up with an answer:

> Gas station danger and media attention have made gas stations the cultural embodiments of American crime and fear.

Her answer is a great start on a thesis or *Slant*.

Take some of the source material you're working with for your essay—whether it be a text, a film, scientific data, cultural phenomena, or even your own life experiences—and start asking some questions now. Here's the rub: After you ask those questions, **answer them.**

2. Blowing Bubbles

Sound juvenile? Don't be so sure. Blowing bubbles is an easy and wonderfully effective exercise in the early stages of topic development. No, it doesn't require high lung capacity.

Write down some topics of interest, even if they're broad. Circle one. Now start to think about things related to that topic. Create a bubble chart of everything you can think of. Remember, all of those related bubbles are prime nuggets of information you can use to generate and clarify your topic. If the topic you start with is general, the connecting bubbles will often be more specific. When you finish, pick a couple that attract you and focus on those.

Take a look at Pablo's first stage of bubbling about his topic of "advantage" in *The Great Gatsby*. He shows us here how to begin. He has created four bubbles that connect to his main idea—the four topics he is most interested in developing.

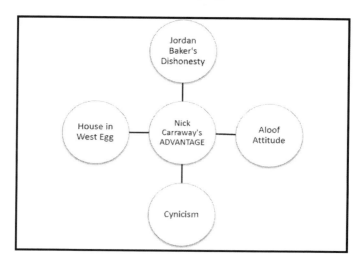

Now, let's look at Jennifer's complete bubbling exercise about gas stations, and particularly gas station crime and fear. Notice how, like Pablo, she has four connecting bubbles to her main topic, and has now developed many connections to those four.

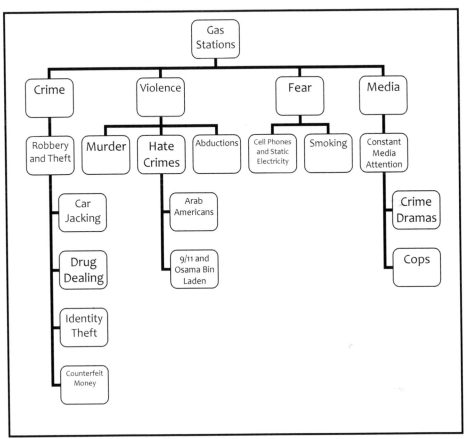

3. Paraphrasing

Paraphrasing will help you both understand the ideas, and articulate a portion of a text.

Choose a passage, perhaps one you've highlighted or marked in the text. Read it over several times carefully. Then translate that text into your own words. Remember, the purpose here is not to summarize, but to interpret. **Your paraphrase should be significantly longer than the original passage.** It's a lot like translating a text from

German (and many texts may read like German to you!). Your job is simply to make sense of it and rewrite it for yourself.

Let's look at Jennifer's paraphrase of a passage from Sophocles' "Antigone." I chose this paraphrase to display Jennifer's close connection to the meaning of the text. Even though Jennifer may have found the meaning distasteful, she kept her own opinion out of it. First, let's look at Sophocles' original passage:

> You ought to realize we are only women,
> not meant in nature to fight against men,
> and that we are ruled, by those who are stronger,
> to obedience in this and even more painful matters.
> (Sophocles 163)

Here's Jennifer's paraphrase:

> You should know that, because we are just women, we're weak against the strength of men. They are born stronger. They rule us, and our role is to obey them and the laws they create. Even when it's painful, we should trust their decisions. (Sophocles 163)

After you've paraphrased a selection of text, review it. Underline words and phrases that represent bigger ideas and themes. Identify the argument and your position.

4. Writing a Dialogue

A dialogue is a great way to test and explore the controversy of a topic. If two people can disagree about a topic, it's a sure sign you have the makings of an argument and a thesis.

Pick a topic. The more specific the better, but if it's broad the dialogue itself will help to narrow it.

Pick two characters. Give the characters a context. For example, if your topic interest is obesity in America, try specifying by placing your characters in a fast food restaurant. Perhaps one is an employee, defending the new nutritious choices the restaurant offers and the new low-fat oil they're using to fry their fries. The second might be an organic food advocate trying to shut the restaurant down.

After you've chosen a context, let the characters argue! Really let each character give the other hell. Have them back up each of their arguments with statistics and examples and details. Let's give it a try:

Jack: I've worked here for fifteen years. When I started, we were flipping burgers for people without a care in the world about their health. Now, we provide nutrition facts for customers, have low calorie and diet options on the menu, and have cut down on trans fats in our cooking.

Cindy: First of all, building jungle gyms in your restaurants to attract kids is shameless. You get them addicted to bad food when they're young and they eat it for the rest of their lives. How can you let yourself be a part of that, Jack? Your commitment to health is so minuscule it's ridiculous! McDonald's is simply responding as trivially as it can to the criticism it's facing.

Jack: Not so. You forget that we give consumers what they want. If they want an underdog while they eat fried potatoes, why shouldn't we give them a swing set and French fries? If they want salad and coffee, we give that to them too. We're not forcing cheeseburgers down anyone's throat here. This place is fun!

Cindy: You forget that providing 99 cent cheeseburgers attracts people who can't afford healthy food. Why don't you have ninety-nine cent organic salads with low-fat dressing?

> **Jack:** Oh! You're not really going to criticize us for providing bargains, are you?

After you're through, take a look at what you've done. Which side are you on? And if you need to narrow your topic, look at the characters' specific responses. Each response should be narrower than the topic, and may be a good way to start focusing. Follow the fear.

In the dialogue above, you could underline specific topics of focus. How about building jungle gyms in McDonald's restaurants? That would be an excellent focus for an essay. How about business responsibility and the price of junk food? How about consumer knowledge about what they're consuming? All of these ideas are good topics to focus on and develop.

5. Playing the Detective

Writing is all about inquiry. So is being a detective. Detectives seek out answers. So do you. Detectives form conclusions based on evidence. So do you. Detectives get wrapped up in intrigue and mystery and danger. So do you.

Pick a topic. Now ask yourself three questions:

1. What are you investigating?
2. What are the clues?
3. Based on the clues, what's your hunch?

Example: Here's a sample detective's report by Jennifer, focusing on the book, *Imperial Life in the Emerald City* by Rajiv Chandrasekaran.

Detective's Report: Imperial Life

1. **What are you investigating?**
   Sex in the United States military. Specifically, how co-habitation, prostitution, gender inequality, and hostile environments affect American soldiers fighting wars.

2. **What are the clues?**
   - "The atmosphere was thick with sexual tension. At the bar, there were usually ten men to every woman. With tours of duty that sometimes stretched to six months without a home leave, some with wedding rings began to refer to themselves as 'operationally single'" (Chandrasekaran 63).
   - "There were prostitutes in Baghdad, but you couldn't drive into town and get laid like in Saigon. There was a persistent rumor of a whorehouse in the Green Zone" (Chandrasekaran 64).
   - War brides from previous wars, such as Vietnam and WWII.
   - Prostitution of native women.

3. **Based on the clues, what's your hunch?**
   The military's atmosphere creates a tremendous amount of sexual tension, especially under the hostile environment of war. Although we don't know the extent to which this tension affects soldiers on an individual level, sex in the U.S. military can be seen as a form of imperialism, especially considering prostitution and war brides. Wars and American occupation in other countries often sexualize other cultures. In addition, women in the military themselves face conflicts with their jobs because of sexual tension. There are many more men than women. This begs the question: do women belong in the military? Or perhaps there needs to be an equal number of men and women. Also, I wonder if hostility adds to lust or a hunger for companionship. Keanu Reeves and Sandra Bullock experience similar tensions when they fall in love in Speed and almost die together. Under normal circumstances, such relationships wouldn't form.

6. "Help! I don't know what the heck I want to write about!"
The Lost Student's GPS

Last resort. Procrastinated too long. Gotta come up with something quick. This one we're pulling out of the confidential files. It's the panacea for all apathy.

It's the random passage.

I like to tell my students that if they choose one page from any book, in five or ten minutes we can all figure out what that book is about. It sounds impossible, but it's amazing what one page of text can offer if you actually take the time to think hard about it and use all your critical thinking skills.

If you're writing about a text, be it fiction or nonfiction, try picking one passage and making it your focus. Perhaps it's a passage you underlined or marked, one you thought was interesting or even baffling. Or maybe you just opened the book, closed your eyes, and swung your pointer finger down. Really! This works!

Now that you have a passage, focus on its meaning. Ask these questions:

---

1. What's it about?
2. Who's it about?
3. Why is the author using these particular words?
4. What does the word choice signify? Are the words poetic? Smooth or harsh? Hot or cold? Confusing or clear?
5. What does this passage say about the rest of the text? Clues?
6. What issues or ideas does the passage suggest? How does that relate to the rest of the story or characters or ideas?

When you answer those questions, your answers may lead you toward a topic. Let's take a look at one of the quotes Jennifer underlined in Sophocles' "Antigone":

> You ought to realize we are only women,
> not meant in nature to fight against men,
> and that we are ruled, by those who are stronger,
> to obedience in this and even more painful matters.

Now let's answer the questions listed above:

1. Well, it's about women accepting their roles as weaker than men. 2. It's spoken by Antigone's sister Ismene to Antigone. 3. The words "nature" and "ruled" and "stronger" and "obedience" are especially telling. 4. With those words we get the sense that Ismene is comfortable with her role as a subordinate female. 5. By the fact that she is telling this to Antigone, and using such strong language, we can infer that Antigone has other ideas and is not comfortable with the role of a subordinate. 6. This passage suggests the ideas of gender, law and rules, conformity, and rebellion against the authority and the status quo.

When you review your answers to the questions, pick out key points that pique your curiosity. I underlined key points and key words in the answer above. With development, each of them could lead to a strong *Slant*.

7.   **Crescendo Analysis**

*star**ting** specific:* Progressive *Inquiry*

The purpose of Crescendo Analysis is to develop an idea by investigating it at different levels or scopes, beginning with a specific detail—a word, a picture, a tweet, or even a paint stroke in Picasso's "Guernica."

Crescendo Analysis can be used for textual analysis or for a more general analysis of cultural artifacts, popular culture, and ideas. Here you will find two sets of instructions—one focused on texts, and the other with more open guidelines.   Each Crescendo Analysis worksheet that follows is also followed by instructions.

CRESCENDO ANALYSIS				Nicholas Leither
STARTING SPECIFIC				
WORD/DETAIL	SOURCE	COMPARATIVE SOURCE(S)	YOUR LIFE/ OBSERVATION(S)	**WORLD**

(Download Crescendo Analysis assignment sheet at www.NicholasLeither.com)

Crescendo Analysis Instructions:

DETAIL

The detail should be the smallest, observable piece of information, and a piece of information that you will use as a reference point for connecting words with ideas. For example, you have found a meaningful tweet on Twitter you'd like to use. Consider choosing one keyword in that tweet first.

Analyze that detail. Record your interpretation of it, and the way it makes you feel (yes, feelings are important). Depending on the detail you choose, research it. If it's a word, look it up in the dictionary (even if you think you know what it means) and record its definition(s). If it's a photograph, carefully study it and make note of the details. If it's a piece of art, do the same. The idea here is to give this one detail time, observation, and deep consideration BEFORE you examine it in context. I challenge you to think small here—to get as molecular as you can in your choices of details.

SOURCE

Now crescendo or zoom out into the source and context of that detail. If you chose a word in a tweet, now it's time to consider the tweet itself and the person who wrote it. If you chose a work of art, now it's time to consider the artist and place it appears—a museum? The web? The side of a building in New York City? As you consider and analyze the source, reference it back to that original detail. How does the source of that detail change or reinforce the meanings of the detail?

COMPARATIVE SOURCE(S)

Zoom out from the source now and connect it to another source. If you chose a tweet, find another tweet from the same author or another author you think connects the ideas. If you chose a work of art, look at other works of art from the same artists and other artists. How do the ideas you developed in the detail and source sections develop as you observe and discover comparative sources?

YOUR LIFE/OBSERVATION(S)

It's at this point where you bring your own observations and connections into the analysis. How do the ideas you have developed and discovered connect with your own life? Your education? Your ideas and discoveries? It's important to be specific here—to lay out a meaningful connection. Perhaps it's an event in your life, a story you can tell that illuminates and explores the issue. Maybe it's something your grandmother once told you, or something you read in a book once that you never forgot. Investigate it, nail it down, and detail the connection.

WORLD

Connect the ideas you've developed to the world—either the world of the detail, your world, or both. For example, if you chose a piece of art from the Renaissance, the world you are exploring here might be historical. On the other hand, it might be interesting to consider how that work of art might connect to and comment on American culture. Just because you're zooming out to the world doesn't mean you can be vague. Focus on examples.

FINISHING

Now try to form complex, paragraph-length questions about ideas you've developed. For example, begin by explaining your idea/position/discovery, quoting the word and the sentence in the text, and forming questions about the implications of your developed idea. Zoom in and zoom out on various points in your crescendo. These questions may serve as thesis questions. You may begin to form a *Slant* by answering them.

For examples of Crescendo Analyses using visuals and other media, please see my website:
www.NicholasLeither.com

Crescendo Analysis for Textual Analysis

CRESCENDO ANALYSIS

Nicholas Leither

STARTING SPECIFIC

WORD	SENTENCE	PARAGRAPH or PAGE	BOOK	WORLD

(Download Crescendo Analysis assignment sheet at www.NicholasLeither.com)

Crescendo Analysis Instructions for Textual Analysis:

WORD

The word should be a "keyword"—a significant or descriptive word, and a word that you will use as a reference point for connecting words with ideas. For example, choosing the word "himself" in Homer's *Odyssey* may not be as helpful as choosing the word "self-possessed."

When you've chosen your word, analyze the word. Record your interpretation of the word, and the way it makes you feel (yes, feelings are important). Look it up in the dictionary too (even if you think you know what it means) and record its definition(s).

SENTENCE

Now crescendo or zoom out into the sentence. Remember, because you chose a "keyword," it's important to interpret and analyze the sentence using the ideas you developed about the word. First, how is

that word used in the sentence? Second, how does the word's meaning and implication fit into the context of the sentence? Third, the word and sentence suggest what ideas? Think sub-textually here. The purpose is to investigate ideas that aren't explicitly stated. What ideas exist "under" the obvious and explicit meanings of the sentence?

PARAGRAPH or PAGE

Zoom out from the sentence to either the paragraph or even the page. How does that sentence fit into the ideas surrounding it? Does your word reappear? How do the ideas you developed in the word section and the sentence section develop?

BOOK

Investigate the book. Look for other words, sentences, and pages in the text that relate to the ideas you've developed. Explain the connections and analyze how those ideas function in the book.

WORLD

Connect the ideas you've developed to the world—either the world of the text, your world, or both. For example, if you're working on Homer's *Odyssey*, how do the ideas you've developed relate to what you know, or can infer, about Ancient Greek culture? And, how do they relate to our world now? Just because you're zooming out to the world doesn't mean you can be vague. Focus on an example.

FINISHING

After you've completed Crescendo Analysis, try to form complex, paragraph-length questions about ideas you've developed. For example, begin by explaining your idea/position/discovery, quoting the word and the sentence in the text, and forming questions about the implications of your developed idea. Zoom in and zoom out on various points in your crescendo. These questions may serve as thesis questions. You may begin to form a *Slant* by answering them.

Example: Lydia's sample Crescendo Analysis follows, focusing on the book *Eating Animals*, by Jonathan Safran Foer:

Crescendo Analysis: Complicity
Lydia Davidson

Word

Complicity (Noun)

According to *Merriam-Webster Dictionary*:
1. The act of helping to commit a crime or do wrong in some way.

The word complicity is used usually to describe people who have allowed for a bad practice to continue. People who are complicit may know what they are doing is wrong, but often rationalize their actions and behaviors. Complicity inspires feelings of guilt, secrecy, and shame.

Sentence

"What is not sufficiently clear, perhaps to any of us, is the extent of our complicity, as individuals and especially as individual consumers, in the behavior of corporations... Most people... have given proxies to the corporations to produce and provide *all* of their food" (Foer 172)

This sentence is part of a quote in Jonathan Safran Foer's book, *Eating Animals*, which originated from *The Art of Commonplace* by Wendell Berry. The word "complicity" used in this sentence accuses Americans of not knowing they are complicit in a large amount of wrongdoing due to our choices. This is a serious accusation because it presents the possibility that as human beings we can do great damage and be complicit in wrongdoing without being aware of it. This sentence discusses complicity in the world of corporate food— allowing food corporations to control how we eat and what we eat, complicit in their exploitation and cruelty.

Paragraph/Page

On this page Foer discusses the idea of "farming by proxy," which Paul Willis, a pig farmer in Thornton, Iowa, introduces to him from *The*

Art of Commonplace by Wendell Berry. Foer discusses how empowering the idea is because it allows the consumer to control and pull the strings. If consumers choose to eat, for example, large quantities of sustainable, organic plants, corporations will supply sustainable, organic plants. Unfortunately, it isn't that simple and every day it is getting harder. Factory farms and industrialized food dominate. There are very few independent, family farms left in America. The longer consumers are complicit, the more power and influence the "goliath of the food industry," factory farms, become.

Book

Foer drops fact after fact about the horrors of animal agriculture. A theme that continuously accompanies those facts is the idea that people do not know and, to some extent, do not want to know how bad the situation is when it comes to their food. It is clear that cruelty is "not only the willful causing of unnecessary suffering, but the indifference to it. It's much easier to be cruel than one might think" (Foer 53). He goes on to say that cruelty "depends on an understanding of cruelty, and the ability to choose against it. Or to choose to ignore it" (53). Complicity is one such way of being cruel.

Foer is well aware of the difficulty of changing one's lifestyle and even more so the lifestyle of a large number of Americans. He often uses anecdotes that show his own struggle with vegetarianism and making the choice to change, not change, or partially change. He tells of how his family life, ethnicity, and childhood impacted those decisions. It is clear that food itself is not the only issue, but how food is connected to social life, culture, and our personal narratives. Foer discusses the idea of "table fellowship" (Foer 55), the social bonding that occurs when people eat together. He knows and acknowledges that our food choices are complex, and that complicity is often rooted deeply in our upbringings, our families, our stories, and the commercial traps set for us by large food corporations who seem to care more about our dollars than they do about our health and their treatment of animals.

World

Complicity in the food industry is this murky gray area that creates conflict and discomfort. In the 2014 documentary *Cowspiracy* by Kip Anderson, complicity was a main theme. Anderson was astounded to discover that environmental agencies and non-profits were avoiding discussing animal agriculture's atrocious effects on the environment and climate change. He found out that there is a fear factor associated with speaking out against agribusiness. Animal agriculture has an incredible amount of power and money. This means that people who accuse and object to the practices of large-scale animal agriculture put themselves in danger of being sued and/or losing funding. In countries with less social stability than the U.S. there is even the possibility of physical harm, such as Dorothy Stang, a nun in Brazil who was killed for her efforts to bring awareness and change to animal agriculture.

The amount of marketing and advertisement aimed at keeping the food industry powerful proves that consumers have trouble thinking for themselves in a climate where powerful food corporations influence every part of the food system. While we often like to think we remain immune from the messages advertisers lay out for us, Dustin Kidd describes the extreme bombardment we are exposed to every day in his book *Pop Culture Freaks*. Whether we want to admit it or not, we are affected by marketing. Seeing Taco Bell and McDonalds and Panda Express on the daily impacts our view of food. Having a common acceptance of eating meat (and lots of it) all the time is a dangerous part of marketing. When something exaggerated becomes the norm, it can be unhealthy and detrimental.

Finishing

How do marketing schemes in the food industry affect socialization and cause complicity? Most people would say that they think of themselves as good people and not people who deliberately cause harm. It is apparent, though, that there are incredible negative effects when it comes to animal agriculture, ranging from severe cruelty against animals to the degradation of our environment through climate change. How do people not see what is happening, and why are they so reluctant to change or acknowledge their own complicity? Moreover, how can Americans and young people, who so often pride themselves on their uniqueness and individuality, be so willing to accept and/or ignore the exploitation of corporate agriculture? Most importantly, how am I responsible, and what am I going to do about it now that I see the truth?

Create

1. Writing a Sentence

It sounds so simple, doesn't it? You've just developed a topic idea in the last section, but you still don't have that core statement that many people call a thesis. Look over your work and try to detect the common idea or core controversy. Forget about forming a complete thesis for now, and instead focus on that core—your *Slant*. What is it that you're exploring in your exercises?

Ask yourself questions. These are *not* rhetorical questions. You're going to answer them here and now. For example, Lydia, after writing her Crescendo Analysis, might ask this question: "Do my food choices make me complicit in the crimes of factory farms, and where do I see that complicity around me?"

That's a good question. But don't stop there. Now, based on your hunch, form an answer. Don't worry about it being right or wrong. Go with your gut. Lydia answered that question this way: "I see the indulgence and complicity the most in our choices and behavior during holidays like Thanksgiving, where we celebrate thanks, love and compassion, but seem to support exactly the opposite in our food choices."

That's a pretty great *Slant*, and it's a topic idea that will eventually lead to a thesis. Start asking and answering your own questions now. Keep asking, "Why?" and "So what?" Have a question and answer conversation with yourself. Write it down or type it on your computer. You might be able to ask a very specific question like Lydia's above, or you may start with something even as silly as this: "Why did I develop this topic?" Here's a sample, based on Jennifer's topic of gas stations from her blowing bubbles exercise:

Question:	Why did I develop the topic of gas stations?
Answer:	Because Lisa Margonelli's book, *Oil on the Brain* interested me in the topic and I can relate to gas stations.
Question:	Why can I relate?
Answer:	Because I use them every week.
Question:	What does that say about me? Do I like gas stations or something?
Answer:	No, not at all. Actually I kind of hate gas stations. They're sketchy as hell, especially at night.
Question:	Why are they sketchy?
Answer:	People rob them all the time. Creeps hang out there. I often feel vulnerable and exposed standing alone in the light. And in those crime shows like *Cops* there are always crimes happening at gas stations.
Question:	Why would that be? Why would criminals flock to gas stations?
Answer:	Because they're open late, and maybe this is out there, but the companies that own gas stations have bad reputations when it comes to the treatment of other people, especially the treatment of less developed nations where they drill for oil.
Question:	I don't get it. What's the connection between the companies drilling for oil and the gas stations that sell it?
Answer:	If a company like Shell acts in a criminal way in Nigeria (Margonelli) to get the oil and represents what many of us would consider immoral and unethical business practices, that criminal aspect will follow that oil through the refinery straight to those gas stations.

Now, look where she began and look where she ended up. Yes, many of you might think that this last statement sounds like a stretch. But I don't think anyone would claim that it's either unoriginal or uninteresting. Jennifer is going long here, pushing boundaries, asking questions and forming answers that are going to take some serious inquiry in order to support. And that is what writing creative essays is all about: Going long. Because Jennifer is interested in the topic, she's setting herself up to write an essay she would want to read.

Right now, start asking yourself some questions and forming answers too, based on your prewriting work from the Rehearse section. What you want to end up with here are several complete sentences much like Jennifer's final answer about Shell and gas stations above. These should be statements of opinion, things that need development and inquiry—something you need to write an essay about to support. Develop a few statements now.

2. Condensing

The key to *Slant* is your opinion. This is your chance to express your opinion about your topic. If your exercise was about the topic of health care, focus on one particular interesting development. Here's what you want to avoid: *Over half the people in America do not have health care.* That may be true, but it's a fact, not an opinion. If that fact interests you, then ask why it's true. That may lead you to an opinion. However, it might also lead you to an observation. Facts and observations are two things that need further development in order to turn them into an argument or a *Slant*. Example:

Fact:	Over half of the people in America don't have health care.
Observation:	The people in America who are lucky enough to have health care are usually the wealthy.
Slant:	The privatization of health care in America makes it a luxury for the wealthy instead of a service equally available to everyone.

This writer came up with his *Slant* by asking himself "So what?" about his observation that most people who have health care in America are wealthy. He is blaming privatization, and will have to prove that the poor often live without health care because of privatization.

Here's an example from Pablo Rocha's early work on his topic about *The Great Gatsby*.

Fact:	Nick Carraway is the narrator of *The Great Gatsby*.
Observation:	Nick Carraway narrates the novel *The Great Gatsby* with an aloof attitude.
Slant:	Carraway's aloof and detached narration and his own admission that he doesn't care what his conduct is founded on exposes his cynicism and his failure to live up to his father's advice to avoid criticizing those who haven't had the advantages he has.

In Pablo's example, you can see how his thinking developed as he dug deeper into his observation.

3. Narrow NOW! Crescendo NOW!
Putting Your Topic on a Diet

In the film *Bowling for Columbine*, by Michael Moore, Moore's primary goal is to figure out why the Columbine killers did what they did. That is a very specific question: Why did Eric Harris and Dylan Klebold massacre thirteen people in their Littleton, Colorado high school? But if you've seen the film, you know that it's about a whole lot more than just Eric and Dylan. It's about rising violence in America.

Many students start with a topic like violence in America. Obviously that's too broad, even for a book. But just because you narrow your topic, doesn't mean that you're abandoning your question about violence in America. That's what Crescendo Analysis is all about. Take a look at the Crescendo Analysis exercise in the Rehearse section. Instead of starting with something broad, general, and/or abstract, you start with something very specific (the Columbine killers) and use it to say something big (violence in America).

One detail or event or statistic can represent much larger themes. Think like Michael Moore. Let a specific question or detail lead you to bigger ideas rather than general and broad ideas leading you to specific ones. Think of an essay like a crescendo. Start carefully and focused. Then grow.

4. Are You Qualified?

One effective way to approach your topic and *Slant* is to ask yourself if you're qualified to write the essay. If not, time to narrow. You may not be qualified to write an essay claiming that Americans are morally bankrupt when it comes to their food choices, and their willing participation in consuming factory farmed animals makes them complicit in the crimes perpetrated by large, food corporations. You're not an expert on food corporations or even ethics and morality. This *Slant* is far beyond your expertise.

However, by narrowing, you almost magically become qualified. When we look at Lydia's Crescendo Analysis about complicity and we look at her *Slant*, we see how she narrowed general complicity down to Thanksgiving dinner with her family, making the argument about herself and her family members instead of generalizing about all Americans.

Lydia's Crescendo Analysis Question: How do people not see what is happening, and why are they so reluctant to change or acknowledge their own complicity?

Lydia's Slant: My family chooses to participate in the consumptive, consumerist rituals surrounding Thanksgiving despite the ethical and cultural contradictions those rituals present to our values, exposing that we are complicit in the consumerism and cruelty in our Thanksgiving meal and holiday.

Do you see how that broad question at the end of her Crescendo Analysis is out of her scope and qualifications as a writer? It's a good question, but who are the people? What are they failing to change? By focusing on *her* choices and *her* family she not only narrows her topic, she allows her family to represent many Americans and many families without having to make broad generalizations about them.

One way to test your topic, *Slant*, and qualifications is to ask yourself this question: "If I were to appear on a televised talk show, and the host asked me questions about my topic, could I answer them with knowledge, authority, and research?" While Lydia would struggle to answer questions about all food corporations and the behavior of Americans, she could easily answer questions about the contradiction between her family's eating habits, and their values.

5. Testing Your Topic Idea
Challenging

The best way to test your statement is to play what Peter Elbow calls in his book *Everyone Can Write* the believing/doubting game, or to try what I call "challenging." The idea is simple. Every argument must have a counter-argument, right? Because your *Slant* is an argument, you need to ask yourself if there's a "challenge." If your *Slant* is what you say, what might someone else say to challenge that idea?

1. Could someone argue with you about your topic? What would *they say*?
2. If your statement is a plus, what's the minus?
3. Offer challenges. You might do this in the form of a dialogue. Here's an example from Jennifer, using her *Slant*:

> **Jennifer's Slant:** In the Greek plays "Agamemnon" and "Antigone," Clytaemnestra's and Antigone's actions are driven by underlying maternal and sisterly instincts.
>
> **Challenge #1:** Both Antigone's and Clytaemnestra's extreme actions are driven by madness and stubbornness, not their sex.
>
> **Challenge #2:** Actually Aeschylus and Sophocles created women characters who were essentially men because they deeply misunderstood the motivations and personalities of women.

Both of these ideas conflict with Jennifer's *Slant*, and therefore prove that her *Slant* is an arguable point and opinion, not merely a fact or observation.

Note: This starts a major theme in *Slant* about developing a "conversation" between your opposition (the challenge) and your *Slant*. The more time you spend clarifying and understanding the nuances of the controversy between opposition and *Slant* here, the easier it will be later on and the less likely you will be to get confused about your own argument. **Don't overlook others' opinions and points of view**.

6. Using *Slant*

If you're having trouble putting all that work you did in the exercises into one or two statements, try getting on the phone. Or better yet, knock on a door. When we force ourselves to explain our ideas to others, we often learn more about ourselves *and* our ideas. Call someone you trust and say, "Hey, does this make sense?" The questions they ask are important and will help you communicate and express your idea. Take notes during the discussion.

2: Writing the Thesis

Approach

1. Pride, Belief and Curiosity

It's time to own it. That's right. *Slant* requires your strong feelings. Your thesis is all yours. It's something you should be proud of. If you're not proud of it by the end of this chapter, it needs more work. Pride, a strong belief, and a sense of curiosity make writing an essay a success. After all the work you put into topic development in the last chapter, you should now have an idea that you feel strongly about. That's the core of your essay. That's your *Slant*.

2. Packing to Unpack

You're about to leave on a road trip into the great unknown. Before you go, however, you need to prepare. What you're about to do with the "although" and three "supported by" statements is pack your suitcase and your car—take all your best ideas, cram them into one duffel, and throw them in the trunk.

Think of your thesis like it's your backpack (a thing that never leaves you) and your outline like it's your duffel. If you pack too much stuff, you're going to be lugging that crap all over the high peaks and dry deserts. If you pack too little, you're going to be too cold, and you're never going to have any clean underwear or dry socks. But if you pack just right, you're going to be fully prepared to have a fantastic trip.

Rehearse

1. Retesting

You've already tested your statement. However, as you know, all experiments undergo several different stages of testing.

The second test is simple (or seems simple). In fact, it's just that one question we need to keep asking ourselves:

So what?

By asking yourself this question you're doing several things. You're asking what implications your statement has on the world. You're also asking how and why it should appeal to readers. And, don't forget, you're asking yourself why you're writing it. Let's see how Pablo was able to transform his *Slant* using this method:

> **Pablo's Draft *Slant*:** Nick Carraway fails to live up to his advice to avoid criticizing others who haven't had the advantages he has.
>
> **So what?** Nick Carraway is the narrator of the novel, and his attitude is often selfish. He admits that after a certain point he doesn't care what his conduct is founded on. He's a cynic, really. He treats the world and the other characters in the novel as though he's above them, looking down. Many readers say that he's fair and kind, but he comes off as very privileged and even judgmental to me.

> **Revised *Slant*:** Carraway's aloof and detached narration and his own admission that he doesn't care what his conduct is founded on exposes his cynicism and his failure to live up to his father's advice to avoid criticizing those who haven't had the advantages he has.

Let's see what Jennifer said when she asked herself that question about her *Slant*:

> **Jennifer's *Slant*:** In the Greek plays "Agamemnon" and "Antigone," Clytaemnestra and Antigone's actions are driven by underlying maternal and sisterly instincts.
>
> **So what?** Often, leaders are accused of being heartless, insensitive, and selfish. Often, these leaders are men. Yet, a tremendous fear of women in power prevails, even in modern-day politics. Perhaps even civilized cultures have an inherent desire to oppress women— confine them to either a domestic setting or a subordinate position in the workplace. But taking into consideration the power of female emotional strength, like Clytaemnestra's and Antigone's, women leaders may provide a refreshing alternative to traditional roles of power. The question now is whether the public is ready to be ruled by women.

Jennifer knows what she wants to prove about Clytaemnestra and Antigone and she also knows what she wants that argument to say about women in powerful roles.

Jennifer's "So what?" turns out to also be her conclusion. This is an interesting thing to keep in mind for later in the essay-writing process. You can often return to your "So what?" as inspiration for your concluding paragraph. Here, Jennifer's "So what?" is too broad for any other part of her essay except her conclusion, which is meant to connect to a broader set of ideas and arguments.

Write your own "So what?" paragraph now.

2. Using Your Own Language

A big part of *Slant* has to do with writing in your own voice, NOT in stilted academic language that you think *sounds* good. Why try to be someone you're not? And why on earth would ever want to write a boring essay?

I know you only have a statement so far, but let's start early. The key to using your own language is reading and writing out loud. Read your statement out loud to yourself now. How does it sound? Confusing? Is it boring? Eloquent? As poetic as Keats? Get used to reading out loud, even if your family and friends and roommates think you're crazy.

3. Subordinate Clauses or "Teasers"

You're about to turn your statement into a subordinate clause—or what I call a "teaser"—using the word "although." The type of subordinate clause we're going to focus on developing here is a sentence that begins with a dependent clause, and ends with an independent clause. Like this:

> **When** *I vote* (dependent clause), *I make a difference* (independent clause).

We call it a subordinate clause because the first portion of the clause (When I vote) could not stand alone as its own sentence. "I vote" could be a sentence, but "When I vote" is dependent. However, the second part of the clause (I make a difference) could stand alone as a full sentence, right?

The first word of the sentence above creates the subordinated structure. That word "when" is called a subordinator. Subordinators allow us to put two separate clauses together into one sentence. Here's a list of common subordinators:

If
As
When
While
Where
Although
Because
Unless
Until

I like to think of the subordinate clause like a mystery gimmick, or a teaser. It keeps readers interested and curious because they have to read the second part of the sentence to understand the first. The dependent clause is a teaser that leads us straight into the independent clause. Try this:

> **Although** many people think evidence in support of Bigfoot is all a hoax, researchers have not conclusively proven the Patterson-Gimlin Film a fake.

Try writing a few teasers now in your own words. Start the sentence with one of the words from the list above.

4. Doing Research

When writing a research essay, you need to find out more about a topic before you're ready to state or specify your opinion. Well now's the time. Go to the library or to the library's website and start looking into your topic. Use the web. The web can be a good starting point for research, and can lead you to solid sources, but don't get in the habit of depending exclusively on Google as your source of research. The best way to begin is to go talk with a librarian.

Create

1. Writing the Opposing Statement

Now that you've put your statement to the test, are following the fear, and have found that it is indeed a *Slant*, write an opposing statement. How would someone challenge your *Slant*? Better yet, find a source. Use the opposing points you came up with in the exercises. If you're arguing that ExxonMobil's devotion to the Global Warming and Energy Project is a case of mere "greenwashing" in order to sell more gas, ask yourself what ExxonMobil would say in their own defense. How would they challenge you? Then do a little research and find out.

Let's take a look at Lydia's *Slant*:

> **My family chooses to participate in the consumptive, consumerist rituals surrounding Thanksgiving despite the ethical and cultural contradictions those rituals present to our values, exposing that we are complicit in the consumerism and cruelty in our Thanksgiving meal and holiday.**

Now let's see what she came up with for an opposition:

> My family argues that Thanksgiving dinner is a time of reflection and a celebration of love, compassion, and community, and that our Thanksgiving rituals and our indulgence in large amounts of delicious food express that love and celebrate our values.

Let's take a look at Jennifer's *Slant*:

52

> **Gas stations embody the American culture of crime and fear.**

Here's her opposition:

> Filling up at the gas station is the hallmark of American consumption and wealth.

Now write an opposing statement to challenge your own *Slant*.

2. Combining *Slant* with Opposition

Start with the word "although." Now, just take your opposition statement and combine it with your *Slant*, like Jennifer has done with both of her statements here:

> Although Clytaemnestra and Antigone, in their criminal pursuit of power and glory, act more like men than women (dependent clause),
>
> **their actions are driven by the female instincts of motherhood and sisterhood** (independent clause).

> Although filling up at the gas station is the hallmark of American consumption and wealth (dependent clause),
>
> **gas stations embody the American culture of crime and fear** (independent clause).

If you have a longer opposition and *Slant*, don't worry. Thesis statements and "although" clauses don't have to be neat or even short. The more details and specific information the better. Notice the details and complexity in Pablo's "although" clause:

> Although Nick Carraway's elegant narration of *The Great Gatsby* may, on the surface, be considered fair, incisive, tolerant, and humble, despite his having come from "well-to-do people" (5),
>
> **Carraway's aloof and detached narration and his own admission that he doesn't care what his conduct is founded on exposes his cynicism and his failure to live up to his father's advice to avoid criticizing those who haven't had the advantages he has.**

Voila! You now have a thesis statement, complete with an opposing argument. You may need to reword it a bit to make it into a coherent sentence—a subordinate clause—but the essence of your argument is now on paper. You have the basic structure and information that will factor into the rest of your outline.

3. Writing the "Supported by" Statements

Now that you have your working thesis, it's time to break it up. The way to do it is simple:

Although [Opposition or Challenge]_____,

[**Your *Slant***]_____.

Supported by_____.
Supported by_____.
Supported by_____.

When you think about your "supported by" statements, think of the ideas that make your *Slant* true in your mind. The "supported by" statements are your "subpoints"—the specific details that will make up the body of your essay. They provide the basis for the support of your argument—the evidence, proof, and examples.

Most writers choose three "supported by" statements, but there is no reason that you can't have more (but you should avoid having only one, even if you're writing a very short essay). The number of "supported by" statements can often correlate to the length of an essay. For example, three works well for a four to eight page essay, but you may find yourself wanting to add another for a longer essay. For now, try three. You can always add another later in the process. Let's take a look at examples from our authors:

Quitting Cold Turkey

Although my family argues that Thanksgiving dinner is a time of reflection and a celebration of love, compassion, and community, and that our Thanksgiving rituals and our indulgence in large amounts of delicious food express that love and celebrate our values,

we choose to participate in the consumptive, consumerist rituals surrounding Thanksgiving despite the ethical and cultural contradictions those rituals present to our values, exposing that we are complicit in the consumerism and cruelty in our Thanksgiving meal and holiday.

Supported by the hypocrisy observed in how we celebrate Thanksgiving like many American families, participate and conform in the rituals, and objectify the animals.

Supported by my family's knowledge about—and disdain for—consumerism, materialism, and the corruption and cruelty that exists in the industrialized food system.

Supported by our reluctance to hear and talk about the food industry, what that might mean when it comes to our Thanksgiving values, and our outright refusal to change our ways based on that knowledge.

Being Innately Woman

Although Clytaemnestra and Antigone, in their criminal pursuit of power and glory, act more like men than women,

their actions are driven by the female instincts of motherhood and sisterhood.

Supported by Clytaemnestra's and Antigone's selfless devotion to their family members.
Supported by Aegisthus's love for Clytaemnestra, which has great influence over her.
Supported by Antigone's righteousness and her intention to do the right thing.

Picking up the Heavy Nozzle—Scary, Right?

Although filling up at the gas station is the hallmark of American consumption and wealth,

gas stations embody the American culture of crime and fear.

Supported by gas station theft and robberies that are on the rise.
Supported by gas station crime escalating into credit card fraud and even hate crimes.
Supported by at-the-pump urban myths causing a certain degree of fear at gas stations.

Notice how Pablo has four "supported by" statements and how he includes textual citations:

A Father's Advice

Although Nick Carraway's elegant narration of *The Great Gatsby* may, on the surface, be considered fair, incisive, tolerant, and humble, despite his having come from "well-to-do people" (5),

Carraway's aloof and detached narration and his own admission that he doesn't care what his conduct is founded on exposes his cynicism and his failure to live up to his father's advice to avoid criticizing those who haven't had the advantages he has.

Supported by his elaborate assumptions about the smallest details, such as Gatsby's unrecognizable silhouette somehow suggesting that he had come out of his house to "determine what share was his of our local heavens" (28).

Supported by his one-sided, journalistic and even voyeuristic obsession with Gatsby, and his abstract and romanticized observations and judgments about his character.

Supported by his distant and clinical hypotheses about Gatsby's love of Daisy and its motivation.

Supported by his link between dishonesty and disadvantage in the case of Jordan Baker, suggesting that those who are underprivileged are therefore dishonest people (74-75).

At first, you might think this is wordy and messy, but that's okay. What Pablo has here is a complete framework for his essay. By the time he writes his draft, this framework will be unpacked and turned into many different paragraphs. For now, it's a packed-tight suitcase. It's better to pack more details and ideas into your thesis and "supported bys" than to rely on generalizations or oversimplifications.

4. Revising Your "Although" and "Supported by" Statements
Avoiding Explaining Your Slant in Your "Supported by" Statements

Now that you have a thesis, let's call it a "working thesis." We do that for a reason. The reason is change. Think of your working thesis as a guide and starting point, not a commandment engraved in stone. The thesis is pliant, and may even be the last thing in your essay that changes.

Reread your work. As you embark on the outline, using what you've already written, it's worth double checking to make sure you have a logical and strong thesis.

One of the main problems to avoid, and the last thing you should check before embarking on the outline, is to make sure you're not explaining your *Slant* in your "supported by" statements. Your "supported by" statements should be very specific subpoints that support—not merely explain—your *Slant*. Take a look at an early version of Pablo's *Slant*:

> Although Nick Carraway's narrative style seems humble and fair,
>
> **Carraway's narration exposes him as a privileged and selfish man.**
>
> **Supported by** his cynicism when describing his own life.
> **Supported by** his failure to live up to his father's advice about not criticizing others.
> **Supported by** his detached narration of Gatsby, and his romanticizing of his character.

Those words "selfish" and "privileged" are too vague to exist alone in Pablo's *Slant*. Because they're too vague, he's forced to pack explanations into his "supported bys" instead of focusing on subpoints. He needs to do a bit more Crescendo Analysis. When he revised, he worked the ideas of cynicism and his father's advice from his "supported by" statements into his *Slant*. Notice, too, how the opposition became more specific and engaging after he narrowed his *Slant*:

> Although Nick Carraway's elegant narration of *The Great Gatsby* may, on the surface, be considered fair, incisive, tolerant, and humble, despite his having come from "well-to-do people" (5),
>
> **Carraway's aloof and detached narration and his own admission that he doesn't care what his conduct is founded on exposes his cynicism and his failure to live up to his father's advice to avoid criticizing those who haven't had the advantages he has.**

Let's look at an early draft of Jennifer's *Slant*:

> Although Clytaemnestra and Antigone, in their criminal pursuit of power and glory, act more like men than women,
>
> **their actions are driven by femininity.**
>
> **Supported by** their sisterhood and motherhood.
> **Supported by** Clytaemnestra's and Antigone's selfless devotion to their family members.
> **Supported by** Aegisthus's love for Clytaemnestra, which has great influence over her and Antigone's sole concern of righteousness and her intention to do the right thing.

Like Pablo's use of the vague words "selfish" and "privileged" in his thesis, Jennifer needs to narrow down that word "femininity." When she revised, she worked sisterhood and motherhood from her first "supported by" into her *Slant*, and broke her last "supported by" into two:

Although Clytaemnestra and Antigone, in their criminal pursuit of power and glory, act more like men than women,

their actions are driven by the female instincts of motherhood and sisterhood.

Supported by Clytaemnestra's and Antigone's selfless devotion to their family members.
Supported by Aegisthus's love for Clytaemnestra, which has great influence over her.
Supported by Antigone's righteousness and her intention to do the right thing.

3: Constructing the Outline

Approach

Outline format and sample outlines are in the Create section of this chapter.

1. "Just Do It": The Outline Method

I know, I know. You dread the outline. The reason you dread the outline is because it's no fun. Writing an outline is like writing a screenplay to a film. The screenplay is the framework. It's the bare bones. But all the life and color and music seem to come in the actual filmmaking.

Well, kind of. The screenplay, just like the outline, has its life and color and music, too. There's a vision in the outline. There's development and logic. There's the framework for a creative work of art. The outline is an essential part of the development process. Don't think of it as the final word on your topic or *Slant*. Think of it as a guide—that *Sherpa* leading you up Everest.

We've all felt overwhelmed when writing essays—we get in so deep and begin to get confused and jumbled. We head off on tangents. We forget our thesis, or *Slant*. We lose perspective. And there's no saving us. We're lost. That's where the outline comes in. It's a reminder and guide. It's that *Lonely Planet* travel guide crammed into your backpack.

In 2010, at Saint Mary's College, I participated in the creation and assessment of a college-wide writing project. In that assessment of hundreds of students' essays, I found that those who wrote outlines overwhelmingly wrote more logical and polished essays. Many of the students who didn't write outlines wrote essays that read more like drafts. They were still struggling to present their ideas logically.

Give it a chance. **Master the outline.** It alone can turn good writers into great ones and struggling writers into strong writers.

Again, let's forget about formal and boring language. An outline is a good place to experiment with language and voice, to experiment with *Slant*. Because the outline is YOUR guide and only YOUR guide, write it for yourself. This doesn't mean that you don't keep the reader in mind—you are a reader—it simply means that there's absolutely no reason to try to sound like someone else. Won't that just confuse you later on? Put it in your own words.

2. Think Complete Sentences

At this point, listing ideas in your outline does you little good. It's time to tune your thinking to the way you speak and write. Everything in your outline should be a complete sentence. This models the writing you'll do in your essay. Some of the sentences in your outline may even appear as topic sentences in your paragraphs.

3. Understanding the Outline's Place
The Outline as Suitcase

As you develop your essay later on, there will be times when you move beyond the outline—when your analysis and logic evolves past what you've already accomplished. That's great. Remember, your outline is a duffel or suitcase. It's the preparation. It's something you pack for the purpose of unpacking.

Rehearse

1. Compiling Support
The Playlist

Whether you're writing a persuasive opinion essay or a research essay, it's time to start gathering and narrowing in on your support. Use your "supported by" statements. Gathering others' opinions and research will help you develop your ideas. Use the library and the web.

Keep a research journal or a research folder/file (online or offline), where you can compile your information. Get in the habit of taking notes so that you remember your sources.

The best way to do this is to start a "Playlist." The Playlist is like a simplified annotated bibliography. It starts with the author's name, includes the title, and is followed by a note about the source and why it's useful to you.

For example, here's a book and a newspaper article in a Playlist:

> Chandrasekaran, Rajiv. *Imperial Life in the Emerald City.*
>
> > A reporter's perspective of the Green Zone and the war in Iraq. Contains a lot of information about how government organizations didn't cooperate, how the Bush administration failed to properly prepare for the aftermath, and the naïve American expectations we put on a foreign country. Note pages 65-79.
>
> Dowd, Maureen. "Escape from the Green Zone." *New York Times* 1 July 2004.
>
> > An editorial pointing out that Americans are "loathed occupiers" rather than "beloved liberators." Paul Bremer sneaks out of Baghdad and the Green Zone with his head down.

2. Writing Pilot Topic Sentences

Before you start the outline, it's a good idea to write some trial or starter statements under the topic of each of your "supported by" statements. Think of them as pilot topic sentences—sentences that include the topic and your *Slant* on that topic. They are like mini thesis statements. Later, you will plug those straight into the outline, but for now, it may be easier to get a head start.

Let's look at a couple pilot topic sentences from Jennifer's gas station topic:

> Overexposure in the media has transformed gas stations' glossy reputation into one of delinquency.

> Advanced crimes have found their way to gas stations, only adding to the aura of paranoia.

> Because gas stations often employ ethnic minorities as clerks, hate crimes have risen; "After 9/11, people who were angry at some vague combination of OPEC and Osama bin Laden attacked a hundred clerks at 7-Eleven gas stations and convenience stores in a month" (Margonelli 11).

Notice that she includes her research in one pilot sentence. This is important in the outline. Research, evidence, and examples can guide the logic of your essay, so get them in your outline. Refer to your Playlist.

Create

1. The Structure

Two things. First, keep it simple. Second, follow the format closely. Barry Horwitz and I spent years working on and tinkering with this outline format. It's designed to not only lay out your essay, but to create a logical foundation for your *Slant*. Don't get carried away with dashes and hyphens and numbers and subpoints under your subpoints. Keep it to numbers with capital letters underneath. When you get too carried away with your outline and cram every bit of knowledge and research into it, your outline becomes overwhelming when writing your essay. Like a screenplay, an outline has a strict format. Follow it.

2. Breaking it Up

You've now written an "although" statement and a few "supported by" statements. Now, as you move into the outline you're going to break up your "although" statement into two parts: Opposition and *Slant*.

For example, here's one of Jennifer's "although" statements with her "supported bys":

> Although filling up at the gas station is the hallmark of American consumption and wealth,
> **gas stations embody the American culture of crime and fear.**
>
> **Supported by** gas station theft and robberies on the rise.
> **Supported by** gas station crime escalating into credit card fraud and even hate crimes.
> **Supported by** at-the-pump urban myths causing a certain degree of fear at gas stations.

She's now going to break up her "although" into two separate statements. Not only that, but she's going to add one "supported by" under her opposition point to suggest support for her challenge. *Support for her opposition? Are you crazy!* Yes, it seems crazy, but remember, in order to present a fair *Slant*, you need to accurately explore another side of the argument. Here's what Jennifer's "although" and "supported by" statements turn into in the outline:

> **Opposition:** Filling up at the gas station is the hallmark of American consumption and wealth.
> > **Supported by** the American economy revolving completely around oil and petroleum products.
>
> **_Slant_: Gas stations embody the American culture of crime and fear.**
>
> **Supported by** gas station theft and robberies on the rise.
> **Supported by** gas station crime escalating into credit card fraud and even hate crimes.
> **Supported by** at-the-pump urban myths causing a certain degree of fear at gas stations.

All Jennifer has done is split up her "although" and added one "supported by" under her opposition. Everything else is exactly the same.

Below is a "before and after" of Pablo's thesis about *The Great Gatsby*. The first shows his thesis before he's split up his "although" and the second shows his thesis after he's broken it into his opposition and *Slant*.

BEFORE:

A Father's Advice

Although Nick Carraway's elegant narration of *The Great Gatsby* may, on the surface, be considered fair, incisive, tolerant, and humble, despite his having come from "well-to-do people" (5),

Carraway's aloof and detached narration and his own admission that he doesn't care what his conduct is founded on exposes his cynicism and his failure to live up to his father's advice to avoid criticizing those who haven't had the advantages he has.

Supported by his elaborate assumptions about the smallest details, such as Gatsby's unrecognizable silhouette somehow suggesting that he had come out of his house to "determine what share was his of our local heavens" (28).

Supported by his one-sided, journalistic and even voyeuristic obsession with Gatsby, and his abstract and romanticized observations and judgments about his character.

Supported by his distant and clinical hypotheses about Gatsby's love of Daisy and its motivation.

Supported by his link between dishonesty and disadvantage in the case of Jordan Baker, suggesting that those who are underprivileged are therefore dishonest people (74-75).

AFTER:

A Father's Advice

Opposition: Nick Carraway's elegant narration of *The Great Gatsby* may, on the surface, be considered fair, incisive, tolerant, and humble, despite his having come from "well-to-do people" (5).

> **Supported by** his describing Gatsby's smile as one that "understood you just as far as you wanted to be understood, believed in you just as you would like to believe in yourself" (62).

<u>*Slant:* Carraway's aloof and detached narration and his own admission that he doesn't care what his conduct is founded on exposes his cynicism and his failure to live up to his father's advice to avoid criticizing those who haven't had the advantages he has.</u>

Supported by his elaborate assumptions about the smallest details, such as Gatsby's unrecognizable silhouette somehow suggesting that he had come out of his house to "determine what share was his of our local heavens" (28).

Supported by his one-sided, journalistic and even voyeuristic obsession with Gatsby, and his abstract and romanticized observations and judgments about his character.

Supported by his distant and clinical hypotheses about Gatsby's love of Daisy and its motivation.

Supported by his link between dishonesty and disadvantage in the case of Jordan Baker, suggesting that those who are underprivileged are therefore dishonest people (74-75).

You'll notice how, after Pablo splits up his "although," he even uses an example from the text of *The Great Gatsby* in his opposition's "supported by." His opposition's "supported by" is more direct and specific than Jennifer's. Remember, messy and specific is much better than vague and oversimplified, right? That's the philosophy of Crescendo Analysis.

Let's now take a look at the complete outline format.

TITLE OF ESSAY

Opposition:_____(counterargument/challenge)_____

    Supported by _____.

Slant: _____(thesis/argument)_____.

Supported by _____.
Supported by _____.
Supported by _____.

_____

1. **Opposition: This sentence should "challenge" your** *Slant.*
   A. *Subtopics, supporting evidence, and explanation for your opposition*
   B. *Complete sentences*

2. *Slant:* **Your thesis statement, argument, in a complete sentence**
   A. *Details and explanation for your thesis. No support here. Explanation only.*
   B. *Complete sentences*

3. **Your first "supported by"**
   A. *Topic sentences that detail out your "supported by" statements*
   B. *Complete sentences*

4. **Your second "supported by"**
   A. *Complete sentences*
   B.

5. **Your third "supported by"**
   A. *Complete sentences*
   B.

3. The Opposition: Number 1

The A's, B's, and C's under number 1 explain the opposition and expand on your opposition's "supported by" statement. Think of them as sentences in a paragraph that will eventually become your opposition paragraph. Use the "supported by" under your opposition to write more specific points here. Here's an example from Jennifer's, "Picking Up the Heavy Nozzle—Scary, Right?" Notice how she uses her opposition's core "supported by," which is "The American economy revolving completely around oil and petroleum products" and provides more specific support in her A and B and C:

---

1. Filling up at gas stations is the hallmark of American consumption and wealth.
   A. Even with prices nearing $4, Americans still consume massive amounts of gasoline because they can.
   B. With the combination of winning lottery tickets, an endless variety of soft drinks and snacks, and little oases of convenience on every corner, Americans are encouraged to spend a lot at gas stations.
   C. Cars are an important part of American culture; "Studies show that people love being alone in their cars more than, say, being at work or at home" (Margonelli 32).

---

4. *Slant*/Thesis: Number 2

Unlike every other section in this outline, the A's, B's, and C's here explain your *Slant*. They do not offer support or evidence for your *Slant*. This is NOT the place to repeat your "supported by" statements. Think of them like sentences in a thesis paragraph. When you get to the actual writing, there will be no thesis sentence. In an essay, there is no such thing as a thesis sentence. There's only a thesis *paragraph* or even thesis *paragraphs*. That's why your A's, B's, and C's are so important here. Find creative ways to explain your argument. You might even try to restate your argument in different words to make it clearer and stronger. You might suggest a comparison, analogy, or metaphor. You might go further into detail.

---

2. Gas stations embody the American culture of crime and fear.
   A. Gas station crimes are not limited to just theft and robbery; they are also places for counterfeit money, abductions, car-jackings, assaults, drug dealing, hate crimes, identity theft etc.
   B. Common knowledge about filling up at gas stations, such as not smoking or talking on a cell phone and touching the car door handle before the gas pump, create uneasiness with gas stations.
   C. The media has increased its coverage of gas station crime, and primetime crime dramas often show gas stations as the scene of the crime.

---

5. The "Supported Bys": Numbers 3, 4, 5...

The best way to think about the A's, B's, and C's under numbers 3, 4, 5... are as topic sentences of separate paragraphs. Break your "supported by" statements up into several sub-points and write topic sentences to represent those ideas. Here's Jennifer's first "supported by" as her number 3:

---

3. Gas station theft and robberies are on the rise.
   A. According to the National Crime Prevention Council, "Recently, there has been increased media coverage across the country regarding theft at gas stations... the unique setting [of gas stations] allows thieves to catch their victims by complete surprise" (NCPC.org).
   B. "Nearly nine percent of U.S. robberies happen in gas stations and convenience stores, and the average gas station lost $1,749 to robbery in 2004" (Margonelli 11).
   C. Hedges eliminate escape routes for would-be robbers, and convenience store gas stations purchase "target hardening kits."

---

6. Three Sample Outlines

Following are two sample outlines from Jennifer and one from Lydia. Use them as guides for your own outlines.

Sample Outline:

Picking Up the Heavy Nozzle—Scary, Right?
Jennifer Tang

Opposition: Filling up at the gas station is the hallmark of American consumption and wealth.

> **Supported by** the American economy revolving completely around oil and petroleum products.

Slant: Gas stations embody the American culture of crime and fear.

Supported by gas station theft and robberies on the rise.
Supported by gas station crime escalating into credit card fraud and even hate crimes.
Supported by at-the-pump urban myths causing a certain degree of fear at gas stations.

---

1. Filling up at gas stations is the hallmark of American consumption and wealth.
    A. Even with prices nearing $4, Americans still consume massive amounts of gasoline because they can.
    B. With the combination of winning lottery tickets, an endless variety of soft drinks and snacks, and little oases of convenience on every corner, Americans are encouraged to spend a lot at gas stations.
    C. Cars are an important part of American culture; "Studies show that people love being alone in their cars more than, say, being at work or at home" (Margonelli 32).

---

2. <u>Gas stations embody the American culture of crime and fear.</u>

  A. Gas station crimes are not limited to just theft and robbery; they are also places for counterfeit money, abductions, car-jackings, assaults, drug dealing, hate crimes, identity theft etc.

  B. Common knowledge about filling up at gas stations, such as not smoking or talking on a cell phone and touching the car door handle before the gas pump, create uneasiness with gas stations.

  C. The media has increased its coverage of gas station crime, and primetime crime dramas often show gas stations as the scene of the crime.

3. Gas station theft and robberies are on the rise.

  A. According to the National Crime Prevention Council, "Recently, there has been increased media coverage across the country regarding theft at gas stations... the unique setting [of gas stations] allows thieves to catch their victims by complete surprise" (NCPC.org).

  B. "Nearly nine percent of U.S. robberies happen in gas stations and convenience stores, and the average gas station lost $1,749 to robbery in 2004" (Margonelli 11).

  C. Hedges eliminate escape routes for would-be robbers, and convenience store gas stations purchase "target hardening kits."

4. Gas station crime escalating into credit card fraud and even hate crimes.

  A. "Using a credit card at a gas station could pose more of a risk for data theft than shopping online, as point-of-sale terminals have emerged as a weak link in the security chain, according to a Gartner Inc. analyst" (Kirk, PCworld.com).

B. Because gas station clerks are typically ethnic minorities, hate crimes have risen at gas stations; "After 9/11, people who were angry at some vague combination of OPEC and Osama bin Laden attacked a hundred clerks at 7-Eleven gas stations and convenience stores in a month" (Margonelli 11).

5. At-the-pump urban myths causing a certain degree of fear at gas stations.

A. Gas stations appear to be explosions waiting to happen. Myths about this include talking on a cell phone and static electricity causing explosions. They are also hazardous to our health, with infected needles being placed under gas pump handles and dangerous fumes.

B. Overexposure in the media has transformed gas stations' glossy reputation into one of delinquency.

C. Crime dramas such as *CSI* and *Criminal Minds* often feature gas stations in the script.

Sample Outline:

Quitting Cold Turkey
Lydia Davidson

Opposition: My family argues that Thanksgiving dinner is a time of reflection and a celebration of love, compassion, and community, and our Thanksgiving rituals and our indulgence in large amounts of delicious food express that love and celebrate our values.

> **Supported by** my family having an overwhelming commitment to each other and an appreciation for table fellowship.

Slant: **My family chooses to participate in the consumptive, consumerist rituals surrounding Thanksgiving despite the ethical and cultural contradictions those rituals present to our values, exposing that we are complicit in the consumerism and cruelty in our Thanksgiving meal and holiday.**

Supported by the hypocrisy observed in how we celebrate Thanksgiving like many American families, participate and conform in the rituals, and objectify the animals.
Supported by my family's knowledge about—and disdain for—consumerism, materialism, and the corruption and cruelty that exists in the industrialized food system.
Supported by our reluctance to hear and talk about the food industry, what that might mean when it comes to our Thanksgiving values, and our outright refusal to change our ways based on that knowledge.

---

1. My family argues that Thanksgiving dinner is a time of reflection and a celebration of love, compassion, and community, and our Thanksgiving rituals and our indulgence in large amounts of delicious food express that love and celebrate our values.
    A. At Thanksgiving dinner, we go around the table and each say something that we are grateful for. Our

meal is very much about appreciating each other and the time that we are spending with loved ones.

B. As a Catholic family, prayer and reflection are a part of our Thanksgiving traditions.

C. We cook and prepare together. The making and eating of Thanksgiving dinner is a joyous family bonding experience.

2. **My family chooses to participate in the consumptive, consumerist rituals surrounding Thanksgiving despite the ethical and cultural contradictions those rituals present to our values, exposing that we are complicit in the consumerism and cruelty in our Thanksgiving meal and holiday.**

A. I am the youngest in my family and the only member of my family without at least a complete bachelor's degree. We are all educated, and cannot use ignorance as an excuse.

B. We recognize the marketing for turkeys and pie and the mass production of food that occurs around the holiday season. My dad and I have had conversations since I was in middle school about the ridiculousness of early holiday marketing in stores.

C. We do not acknowledge the clear contradictions that exist around the Thanksgiving holiday, and instead ignore them in order to indulge.

3. The hypocrisy observed in how we celebrate Thanksgiving like many American families, participate and conform in the rituals, and objectify the animals.

A. We wake up and watch Macy's Thanksgiving Day Parade. Even just the name promotes consumerism and materialism.

B. We make little turkeys out of coffee filters, objectifying turkeys and turning them into commodities for us to consume instead of living animals.

    C. We cook one or two turkeys, mashed potatoes, cranberry sauce, stuffing, pumpkin pie, and pecan pie with no knowledge about where any of that food came from and how it was raised.

    D. As we claim to be celebrating the importance of family and giving thanks, football games are on in the background as we cook and eat.

4. My family's knowledge about—and disdain for—consumerism, materialism, and the corruption and cruelty that exists in the industrialized food system.

    A. My parents and I discuss, often in an abstract and generalized way, how materialistic Americans have become relatively often.

    B. My mom buys organic food and shops at places like Sprouts and Trader Joe's in order to get better quality food, showing that she does value quality, health, sustainability, and humane treatment of animals.

    C. How does my family react to the fact that 46 million turkeys are eaten in the United States on Thanksgiving, and how do they rationalize the misery of their lives on factory farms? (Foer 247-252).

    D. *Note: Using information from Jonathan Safran Foer's Eating Animals, I will ask my family about their awareness and knowledge about factory farms and the industrialized food system.*

5. Our reluctance to hear and talk about the food industry, what that might mean when it comes to our Thanksgiving values, and our outright refusal to change our ways based on that knowledge.

    A. Dinner conversation gets extremely tense if the food industry and how it affects Thanksgiving is brought up. The topic is taboo, causes discomfort, and disrupts the rituals and patterns.

    B. Vegetarians and vegans are often seen as weird and unnatural. Whenever I invite vegetarian or vegan

friends over my dad or brother make some sort of
disparaging comment.

C. There is no amount of information that could change
my father's or brother's minds. When my parents
jokingly told my brother that we were having
Tofurkey for Thanksgiving dinner, he said, "No way."

D. Note: *Much of this section is going to rely on my
observations over Thanksgiving break.*

Sample Outline:

Being Innately Woman
Jennifer Tang

Opposition: Clytaemnestra and Antigone, in their criminal
pursuit of power and glory, act more like men than women.
  Supported by the aggressive strength, independence
  and even appearance of both characters.

**Slant: Clytaemnestra's and Antigone's actions are driven by the
female instincts of motherhood and sisterhood.**

Supported by Clytaemnestra's and Antigone's selfless
devotion to their family members.
Supported by Aegisthus's love for Clytaemnestra, which has
great influence over her.
Supported by Antigone's righteousness and her intention to
do the right thing.

1. Clytaemnestra and Antigone, in their criminal pursuit of
power and glory, act more like men than women.
    A. Clytaemnestra "speaks like a man... full of self-
    command" (Aeschylus 116) and her watchman

says she is "full of high hopes. That woman— she maneuvers like a man" (Aeschylus 103).

B. Creon believes that a man committed the forbidden burial (Sophocles 172) and Antigone refuses her sister's advice not to fight against men (Sophocles 163).

C. Both women are incredibly strong and independent; most Greek women cannot or refuse to defy the law.

D. Clytaemnestra and Antigone are stark contrasts to traditionally admired women in Greek mythology, such as Penelope and Helen.

2. Clytaemnestra's and Antigone's actions are driven by the female instincts of motherhood and sisterhood.

A. Clytaemnestra did not murder Agamemnon for his power, but to bring justice for the untimely death of her daughter.

B. Antigone did not bury her brother because she wanted to defy Creon or win the city's sympathy, but to fulfill her divine duty and pay her last respects to her brother.

C. Antigone's and Clytaemnestra's motives shed light on the inferior motives and weakness of the men in their lives, such as Creon, Agamemnon, Haemon, and Aegisthus.

3. Clytaemnestra and Antigone are selflessly devoted to their family members.

A. Clytaemnestra fails to protect her daughter from Agamemnon, who "thought no more of [sacrificing Iphigeneia] than killing a beast" (Aeschylus 162). This brings great distress for Clytaemnestra, as Iphigeneia is "the agony I laboured into love" (Aeschylus 162).

B. Clytaemnestra's loveless marriage causes her to latch onto her child's love and when Agamemnon

took that away, "he brutalized [her]" (Aeschylus
163).
C. Antigone believes "It is not for Creon to keep me
from my own" (Sophocles 163) and she is to
provide her brother with a proper burial no
matter what.
D. Antigone risks death because it is her instinct to
care for loved ones.

4. Clytaemnestra is influenced by her love for Aegisthus.
    A. Aegisthus encourages Clytaemnestra to murder
because he wants to share the throne. Although
Clytaemnestra inherits the throne after
Agamemnon's death, she says "If I fall, the
throne is yours" (Aeschylus 163).
    B. With her husband gone and her other children
doubting her, Aegisthus is the only one who is
"loyal... as always" (Aeschylus 163).

5. Antigone is righteous and her only purpose is to do the
right thing.
    A. While men only care about winning or losing (Ex:
Creon says, "we must not let people say that a
woman beat us" [Sophocles 183]), Antigone just
wants to do the right thing. She "knows I am
pleasing those I should please the most"
(Sophocles 164).
    B. Creon cares too much about public opinion and
Antigone doesn't care at all. She only cares about
whom divine law deems most important— her
family members, showing that her priorities are in
the right place.

4: Beginning Your Draft: Writing the "Trifecta"

Approach

1. Undoing It

Imagine: You're at a party. Someone you barely know walks up to you and says, "Gas stations are the cultural embodiment of American crime and fear" or "Clytaemenstra's and Antigone's actions are driven by the female instincts of motherhood and sisterhood."  It's ridiculous. If you don't tell them to get the heck out of your face, you might ask them what the heck they're talking about, right?

Well, why should we have different expectations for an essay? When you hammer your opinion down a reader's throat, you're putting them off before you even get started. Not only that, but if you rush to your opinion, stating your *Slant* up front and in one sentence, who's going to remember it? Who's able to process an entire, complex thesis in one sentence at the beginning of an essay? It's asking the reader to do far too much work and to trust your opinion before you've earned it.

The reason some teachers have instructed you to repeat the thesis in your conclusion is because no one is able to process the information in a thesis sentence in the first paragraph of an essay. It's a prescribed cure for an illness that doesn't have to infect your writing. If you need a reminder about the thesis—the very core and purpose of the essay—by the time you reach the conclusion, something is terribly wrong. By the time a reader reaches the end of your essay, not only should he or she understand your *Slant*, he or she should be able to tell someone else about the points that support it.

Now, imagine this: You're at a party and a young woman comes up to you. She asks you if you've ever considered the role of women in Greek mythology. Then she talks a bit about how Clytaemnestra and Antigone are often considered, by many readers, masculine, with aggressive personality traits that mirror that of male heroes. And then, finally, she states her *Slant*, "But I think Clytaemenstra's and Antigone's actions are driven by the female instincts of motherhood and sisterhood."

You'd be less likely to tell that person to get out of your face, wouldn't you? And you'd be a lot more engaged and knowledgeable about her *Slant*, right? That's how we get to the Trifecta.

2. Unpacking the Opposition and *Slant* into the Trifecta

 You've now driven into new territory or you've landed in a strange land. You're holding your carry-on in your hand and your duffel bag is hanging from your shoulder. You took a cab to the hotel, and you just unlocked the door. Although a bit weary and jet-lagged, you're excited to begin exploring the unknown. Time to start unpacking.

To be specific, the Trifecta is the first three-part unit of your essay. It can often be a three-paragraph unit, too, but it doesn't have to be. For now, let's keep it simple and think about it in terms of a three-paragraph unit. We'll discuss ways of changing and expanding it later. The structure is simple. The first paragraph is an opening, the second your opposition, and the third your *Slant*. Three paragraphs, unpacked from your outline that begin your first draft.

The first paragraph, or opening, introduces the topic of your essay, but doesn't yet take a side. It remains neutral. Its purpose is to prepare your readers for the topic you're writing about and engage their interest and curiosity. Opening paragraphs can be personal stories or anecdotes, summaries, a compilation of facts or statistics, or even an explanation of one shocking statistic. The opening paragraph does not appear in your outline. It's something you generate when you write (and you may even decide to write your opening paragraph last).

The second paragraph is your opposition or counterargument. But remember, just because you're writing an opposition paragraph doesn't mean that the opposition only appears in that paragraph. The opposition paragraph is a lot like the thesis paragraph—it introduces an argument you're going to explore in greater detail in your essay. Many essays turn out to be "conversations" between opposition and argument all the way through. A lot of students wonder why it's necessary to provide the opposition in the first place. There are two main reasons. The first is to show the reader that you're knowledgeable about your topic and a fair arguer. The second reason is to make *your* argument legitimate and clearer to the reader. The whole purpose of the Trifecta is to set up your *Slant*. By showing the reader the opposition, your *Slant* is highlighted and clarified.

The third paragraph is your thesis paragraph, or *Slant*. Now that you've created a one-sentence *Slant*, forget about keeping it around. Think more in terms of a paragraph. Like your opposition, your thesis paragraph is devoted to **explaining** your *Slant*. You don't need to state your thesis in one sentence. Your *Slant* paragraph is there to set up your argument. Resist the urge to include your "supported by" statements in your thesis paragraph. They will form the entire body of your essay.

Let's take a look at a sample Trifecta from a professional writer named David Owen, who wrote the article "The Inventor's Dilemma" for the May 17th, 2010 issue of *The New Yorker*. Below is the first page of that article. Pay close attention to what he's doing in the first three paragraphs.

From: *The New Yorker*, May 17, 2010

The Inventor's Dilemma

An eco-minded engineer discovers the limits of innovation

By David Owen

In 2004, while Saul Griffith was a Ph.D. student at the Massachusetts Institute of Technology, he won a thirty-thousand-dollar award that is given each year to a student who has shown unusual promise as an inventor. Griffith was an obvious candidate. Neil Gershenfeld, one of his professors, described him to me as "an invention engine," and said, "With Saul, you push 'Go' and he spews projects in every imaginable direction." The judging committee was especially impressed by a device that Griffith had created to custom-manufacture low-cost eyeglass lenses, intended primarily for people in impoverished countries.

Traditional lensmaking is a process involving thousands of costly molds. Oversized lens blanks are cast in plastic, and then technicians grind and polish them to match individual prescriptions. Griffith told me, "I wanted to make a machine that would negate the need for that entire factory—to let you print the lenses on demand." So he built an inexpensive desktop device with which a minimally trained operator could turn a fast-hardening liquid into a finished lens in a few minutes. The machine had a single, universal mold, with an adjustable metal ring—like a tiny springform cake pan—between a pair of flexible membranes, whose degree of convexity or concavity could be controlled by a simple hydraulic system. "Literally with only those two inputs—the shape of your boundary condition and the pressure—you can define an infinite number of lenses," Griffith explained. That year, he won a five-hundred-thousand-dollar MacArthur Fellowship—a "genius grant"—and the MacArthur judges cited the eyeglass invention as having "the potential to change the economics of corrective lenses in rural and underserved communities around the world."

But winning prizes turned out to be easier than changing the world, and Griffith's lens printer has never found a market. "It turned out that we were solving the wrong problem," he told me recently. "A lens factory is expensive to build and equip, but once you've got one you can make lenses cheaply, and then you can deliver them anywhere in the world for a dollar or two in postage." In effect, Griffith's invention addressed a problem that had been solved years before, at lower cost, by Chinese labor and global shipping. The real problem with eyeglasses in the developing world isn't making lenses, he told me; it's testing eyes and writing accurate prescriptions for people with little or no access to medical care—a matter of politics and economics rather than technology.

David Owen's first paragraph is a neutral opening to the essay—a brief history about the subject of the essay, Saul Griffith.

His second paragraph is his opposition, in which he states the perspectives of the MacArthur judges—that Griffith's invention is so important that it has "'the potential to change the economics of corrective lenses in rural and underserved communities around the world.'" Therefore, the "challenge" in Owen's essay claims that Saul Griffith's invention will change the world.

But then comes his third paragraph, his thesis paragraph, or *Slant*, in which he writes: "But winning prizes turned out to be easier than changing the world, and Griffith's lens printer has never found a market." He goes on to state in that paragraph that the problem with eyeglasses is "a matter of politics and economics rather than technology."

Pretty elegant, isn't it? For many of us, writing the Trifecta is a difficult step because we're so used to jumping straight into our own arguments and ideas. However, it's now time for you to consider "the other," and construct an essay that creates a "conversation" between your argument and others' perspectives.

You're at that critical stage in your writing when you're ready to compose an essay just like a professional writer would. The Trifecta is the key.

3. Flexibility

Remember Jackson Pollock? The artist who splattered paint on his canvases? Breaking the rules made Jackson Pollock famous, but that doesn't mean that he didn't first master the fundamentals of drawing and painting. So before you decide to start throwing words and sentences and paragraphs at your paper, master the fundamentals of the Trifecta.

Once you perfect the Trifecta, it's up to you how you use it. For example, sometimes, if your opposition provides a good hook, you may not need an opening paragraph and can instead use your opposition as both an opening paragraph and opposition paragraph. If your opposition is difficult and complex, you may need more than one paragraph. If you're writing a long research essay with a complicated thesis, you may need to extend your thesis paragraph into two, maybe even three, paragraphs.

Creativity, common sense and logic are the best ways to approach the Trifecta. The Trifecta is the foundation for your essay. If it's faulty, the whole building is going down.

4. Writing Out Loud

Because you want to keep your writing fresh and conversational, write out loud. Instead of reading what your fingers type onto the page, **tell** them what words to type. It's an easy way to make sure you're being clear and conversational, that you're using your own particular style and *Slant*.

Rehearse

1. Impressing Someone at a Party

The best way to start thinking about the Trifecta is to imagine yourself starting a conversation with a stranger about your topic. The Trifecta has a natural conversation-starting structure. Imagine that you're at a party, where you're surrounded by a bunch of crazy-smart people you want to impress. You don't know anybody very well and you want to make some contacts. You need to "pitch" them your idea and make it sound engaging so they ask you more about it and start a conversation.

For example, let's see how Lydia uses her "although" statement and turns it into a Trifecta-esque conversation about Thanksgiving:

> **Opening:** "Have you ever thought about having Tofurkey instead of turkey at your family Thanksgiving?"
>
> **Opposition:** "I don't know about you, but in my family, Thanksgiving is about the food, sure, but it's mostly about togetherness, love, and compassion."
>
> *Slant:* "But you know what we do? We watch football, celebrate mass consumption by overeating and watching the Macy's Parade. That turkey on our table? It spent its entire, short life in misery for us to consume. So, if you just looked at our Thanksgiving by observing our actions, choices, and behaviors, you wouldn't see compassion. You'd see a family complicit in consumerism and animal cruelty."

Notice how each of these statements build off the last? That's an important part of the Trifecta. Though it's three separate paragraphs, it's also a cohesive unit.

Now, let's go backwards from David Owen's Trifecta in "The Inventor's Dilemma" from *The New Yorker* and turn it into a three-part conversation starter:

> **Opening:** There's this famous young inventor named Saul Griffith who has won all these awards for inventing low-cost eyeglass lenses. Ever heard of him?
>
> **Opposition:** Even the judges of the MacArthur fellowship Griffith won believed that his invention would "change the economics of corrective lenses in rural and underserved communities."
>
> **Slant:** However, "Griffith's lens printer never found a market" because the real problem in the eyeglasses business is testing vision and writing prescriptions for people with "little or no access to medical care."

Write your own conversation starter using the Opening, Opposition, *Slant* structure now.

Create

1. Writing Order

There's no right or wrong way to approach the writing order of the Trifecta as long as you can create a clear, logical and strong three-part unit that forms the framework of your essay. For example, you may not yet be ready to write an opening paragraph. That's okay, as long as you do it eventually.

Others, however, may want to at least write a working opening paragraph. Remember, in writing an essay, everything is flexible and subject to change. Just because you write something now, doesn't mean you can't change and rewrite it later, right?

2. Writing the Opening Paragraph

Your primary goal here is to interest the reader. There are thousands of ways to do this. Some popular openings are stories or anecdotes, shocking and attention-grabbing statistics, questions, or examples.

But you should never focus your opening on something you never return to in your essay. If you tell a personal anecdote in your opening and you never return to that anecdote in your essay, the opening feels gimmicky and contrived. Let's take a look at Jennifer's opening paragraph for her essay about gas stations.

> I was only sixteen and it was my very first time. Though I had come to this place a thousand times before, I was scared and unsure whether I knew how to do it right. I was now going to fill up a gas tank by myself. Steven, my driving instructor, had already taught me how to weave through thick downtown traffic and maneuver steep hills, but going to the gas station made me uneasy. We pulled up to a Chevron in a neighborhood full of pastel-colored homes and family-owned restaurants; it was shiny, clean, and the sun glistened off the sharp steel edges of the gas pump. As I nervously picked up the heavy nozzle, Steven explained in his broken English the steps to "fill 'er up": Hand the clerk two $20 bills, place the nozzle in the car, lift the handle, push the button, and watch the digital numbers stir. The process was very mechanical. Before I knew it, Steven's double-pedaled Corolla was ready to go. I took a sip of my Coke from the convenience store, feeling extremely relieved, but I didn't know why. That hot summer afternoon was the day I officially became a small part of America's massive oil culture.

Jennifer's opening is a personal anecdote, and the reason she chose that anecdote is because she uses herself as an example in her essay in order to support her *Slant*. Notice how she varies her language and uses descriptive terms like "shiny" and "clean" and "glistened" to give the readers a visual of the gas station. Notice too how her last sentence delivers the bigger picture, telling us how her opening functions in the larger world of her essay.

3. The Opposition Paragraph

For many students, this is the hardest paragraph to write. Many feel uncomfortable giving the opposition a chance. By offering the reader an opposition you're showing him or her that you know the issues and you're a fair writer.

What most writers seem to forget about the Trifecta, and specifically the opposition, is that the three-part unit works to clarify and solidify your *Slant* in the readers' minds. Your goal is to use the opposition to make your thesis paragraph clearer and stronger. By understanding the challenge to your *Slant*, your reader understands your *Slant*. Don't forget the logic of the party conversation presented earlier. Play the devil's advocate. Step out of your own shoes and consider the other's perspective. Here's Jennifer's opposition paragraph about gas stations:

> Like taking the SATs or going to the prom, filling up at the gas station for the first time has become a milestone for every American teenager. Part of the United States' identity is rooted in the ideal that every American can own a car—a revolution sparked by Henry Ford's Model T. For many Americans, driving their cars is an inherent part of everyday life. Going to the gas station is equivalent to the French running to the bakery for a baguette. Driving is our identity. Accelerating on an open highway captures American freedom in its truest form and "studies show that people love being alone in their cars more than, say, being at work or at home" (Margonelli 32). Gas stations act as pseudo concierge services that offer winning lottery tickets and an endless variety of soft drinks and snacks to maximize the driving experience. Other nations have monarchies, monuments, and museums to represent their country. Americans have cars. Gas stations are the backbone of America's rich and prosperous identity—the castles full of liquid gold and black jewels that keep our nation running.

4. The Thesis Paragraph

This is the most important paragraph of your entire essay. It's the core of your *Slant*. It's best to write a working thesis paragraph before you write your essay, and return to it over and over as you write and revise. The thesis paragraph, like the thesis statement itself, is flexible. **It's one of the first things you write and one of the last things you revise.**

The purpose of your thesis paragraph is not to cram in every point you plan to cover. The purpose is to make your argument, your *Slant*, clear. The first thing to keep in mind is transitioning from your opposition paragraph. Somehow you need to make it clear that you're making a distinction between what you stated in your opposition paragraph and your own *Slant* in your thesis paragraph. What you don't want is to sound like one moment you think one thing and the next minute you think another.

Sometimes, one word can help. Jennifer uses the word "however." David Denby, in another example that follows from *The New Yorker*, uses the word "nevertheless." David Owen in the previous example uses the word "but." These are common transition words between ideas. Other words and phrases are: "yet," "contrarily," "conversely," "on the other hand," "even so," and "even though." Sometimes we need a word or a phrase or a sentence to indicate that we're switching gears.

Here is Lydia's thesis paragraph for her essay, "Quitting Cold Turkey." She uses sentences to switch gears from her opposition and expose the controversy. See how it works:

> This is the underlying problem in my family's Thanksgiving. Yes, we do have values. We value family, friendship, love, honesty, and compassion to name a few. However, these values seem to contradict what we actually end up supporting on Thanksgiving. Worse than that, we *know* that there is a problem with the food we are eating and how Thanksgiving is celebrated through the unabashed buying and selling of everything possible. If we did not know, maybe we would have an excuse. But we do. We know it. And it makes us complicit in the corruption. We are failing to take responsibility for the fact that we are participating in Thanksgiving in a way that supports cruelty, consumerism, and corporate greed, all of which directly oppose our explicit values.

5. Sample Trifectas

Now, let's look at the first three paragraphs—the Trifecta—of Jennifer's essay, "Being Innately Woman." Notice how she follows the party conversation method. She opens with a discussion of women in Greek mythology, ending her opening paragraph with a question that is then discussed in her opposition and thesis. She also incorporates the text into her Trifecta.

In Greek mythology, Helen, Penelope, and Jocasta represent the objects over which men fight wars, the loyal wives to whom brave warriors return, and unknowing, helpless wives and mothers. Throughout Greek texts like the *Odyssey* and "Oedipus the King," women are portrayed traditionally—as vulnerable, as conformists, and as dependent. Characterized as idle creatures, Greek women often commit their loyalty and submit their freewill to the likes of men. According to the character Ismene in Sophocles' "Antigone" women are "not meant in nature to fight against men, / and [they] are ruled, by those who are stronger" ("Antigone" *lines* 71-72). However, two women defy these female norms. Clytaemnestra and Antigone challenge the limitations of their gender and become models for modern-day feminism. They refuse to conform to the conventional roles of women in Greek mythology, but does this make them any less womanly?

Much of Clytaemnestra's and Antigone's strengths are credited to the notion that they have masculine personalities. Clytaemnestra speaks "like a man ... full of self-command" ("Agamemnon" *lines* 355-356). Even Creon, the king in "Antigone," suspects a "man who with his own hand did the [illegal] burial" when Antigone, a young woman, proves to be the culprit ("Antigone" 337-338). Because they do what typical women cannot or refuse to do, readers often perceive Clytaemnestra and Antigone as less womanly. Readers rationalize their deviant behavior by believing that Clytaemnestra and Antigone are motivated by their unorthodox, masculine personalities. For instance, the Watchman tells Clytaemnestra, "So she commands, full of her high hopes. / That woman—she manoeuvres like a man" ("Agamemnon" 12-13). And Antigone refuses to take her sister's advice when she fights against men, despite it being against a woman's nature ("Antigone" 71). A greed for power and a lust for glory spur men to commit their crimes. Therefore, Clytaemnestra and

Opening

Opposition

Antigone are out of tune with the female norms of compassion and loyalty that define other women in Greek mythology, like Penelope.

However, Clytaemnestra and Antigone, though untraditional, bolder, and more radical, are no less compassionate, loyal, or loving than other women in Greek mythology. They are not men, nor are they trying to be like men; rather it is the very core of their womanhood that leads them to commit their crimes. Maternal and sisterly instincts drive Clytaemnestra and Antigone to aggressive actions. After all, a mere man like Aegisthus would not have murdered a war hero just to avenge the death of a daughter. A young man like Haemon would not have defied the king simply to fulfill a divine family duty. Clytaemnestra does not murder her husband, Agamemnon, because of a masculine greed for power. No, she murders her husband because of female grief and a desire for vengeance on behalf of her murdered daughter. Antigone does not bury her brother because of a boyish rebellious nature or a hunger for glory. No, she rebels in order to fulfill her divine duty as a sister and to pay respect to a beloved, fallen brother. Neither woman deserves to be accused for taking on roles unnatural to them. Instead, Clytaemnestra and Antigone deserve to be celebrated for embracing their primal, womanly instincts and obligations fully, even if it means personal doom.

Now, let's look at a very sophisticated "Trifecta" from another professional writer from *The New Yorker*—a film critic named David Denby. You'll notice something odd about it immediately. It only has two paragraphs. But how can you have a Trifecta with only two paragraphs? Take a look:

From: *The New Yorker*, May 31, 2010

The Current Cinema

Epic Struggles
"Prince of Persia" and "John Rabe."

by David Denby

Opening &
Opposition

The producer Jerry Bruckheimer has turned himself into a digital Cecil B. De Mille, a man who was notable for the bizarre and often pointless munificence of his projects. Yet you have to give Bruckheimer credit, of a sort, for successfully coaxing TV-bound families out of their homes with his wildly redundant productions. In the most recent "Pirates of the Caribbean" slosher, he and the director, Gore Verbinski, poured on two hours and fifty minutes' worth of ice floes, waterfalls, steam, and slime—the cinematic equivalent, for those who actually stayed through the picture, of a banana split with added scoops of Dulce Delish, Adirondack Bear Paw, and Boston Cream Pie. Now, for "Prince of Persia: The Sands of Time," based on the video game of the same name, Bruckheimer has spent an estimated hundred and fifty million dollars constructing, among other things, sixth-century Persian palaces (or, at least, their façades) in Morocco, complete with towers, terraces, passageways, and arches. Hundreds of hours in museums and libraries were devoted to scrutinizing Persian weaponry and décor, to produce authentic replicas of scabbards and scimitars, not to mention drapes, carpets, and filigreed wall decorations. A movie like this is a boon to honest craftsmen; some workers, instructed to age a newly sewn costume, attacked it with a cheese grater.

Thesis
Paragraph
Slant

Nevertheless, apart from some sensuous Moroccan desert dunes, the movie looks like schlock. The interiors, which were shot in a London studio, are based on Victorian Orientalist paintings in which people in robes crowd around some potentate or a lolling Scheherazade. But why copy second-rate academic works that linger in the unvisited galleries or basements of the world's museums? These pictures have become, at best, culturally disreputable curiosities. (Hint to moviemakers: if you want to film nineteenth-century Western notions of the Orient, do it as parody, or as something stylized, as Fritz Lang did in 1959, with "The Indian Tomb," one of his mad final movies.)

Not every Trifecta was created equal. Remember, the Trifecta is an idea, not a formula. Jennifer decided to break up her thesis paragraph into three paragraphs in her essay about gas stations. David Denby uses his opposition as an opening. Every writer needs to take the idea of the Trifecta and turn it into a working unit in his or her essay. If it's three paragraphs, fine. If you decide you're going to use your opposition as an opening, as David Denby does above, fine. If you decide you need two or even three paragraphs of opposition, fine.

Professional writers like David Denby use the Trifecta in order to avoid seeming like someone who is too quick to judge—too brazenly opinionated. Imagine if the first sentence of his essay was the first sentence of his thesis paragraph: "Apart from some sensuous Moroccan desert dunes, the movie looks like schlock." It's too aggressive. It sounds overly arrogant. The Trifecta allows the writer to gradually, logically build up to his or her *Slant*, and express alternative points of view.

It's an elegant and effective technique. However, just because you insert an alternative perspective (opposition) into a paragraph in the Trifecta, does not mean that you abandon your opposition entirely in the rest of the essay. The Trifecta sets up a "conversation" between ideas in your essay, and if you fail to offer other perspectives anywhere in your essay, you're going to come off as arrogant, biased, and narrow. What many students say when writing opposition points is something like this: "But it weakens my argument!" However, every reader who has ever critically read an essay knows that considering others' perspectives never weakens the writer's argument unless the writer is clearly wrong. Don't be afraid of the opposition. Just follow that fear.

Lastly, let's look at Pablo's trifecta. Because Pablo is working on a longer essay, he has a longer Trifecta. Most importantly, notice how he has two opposition paragraphs and two thesis paragraphs:

A Father's Advice
Advantage and Privilege in *The Great Gatsby*
By Pablo Rocha

When it comes to privilege, most of the time there's no middle ground. You are either born with a long and steady downhill you can coast right down, or you are born facing a steep uphill you have to climb. That long steady downhill appears right there on the first page of F. Scott Fitzgerald's *The Great Gatsby*. The first-person narrator, Nick Caraway, reveals that his father once told him, "'Whenever you feel like criticizing anyone ... just remember that all the people in this world haven't had the advantages that you've had'" (3). The message is this: If you coast downhill, you better think twice before judging the climbers.

Nick Carraway is a coaster. He often comes off to the reader as a humble, moderate, and fair character, accepting the fact that he came from "prominent, well-to-do people" (5). He narrates the book with an objective and rational point of view. He is capable of self-assessment, and can admit that he has faults. After suggesting that his father taught him a sense of "tolerance," he admits that "it has a limit" (4).

Even Carraway's observations of Gatsby, who is the source of much gossip and rumor, are often balanced, careful and incisive. When Carraway first meets Gatsby he describes his smile as one that "understood you just as far as you wanted to be understood, believed in you just as you would like to believe in yourself" (62). Just as his father advised, Nick Carraway suspends his judgment of this man so that he can get to know him closely throughout the story. His language and perspective suggests that he is spared the moral corruption that often comes with privilege.

The problem has to do with that word "advantage." Nick Carraway's privilege has allowed him his detachment. His "advantage" as the narrator is to be so aloof that he doesn't have to climb, doesn't have to take risks, and can be comfortable in his detached observations of the various silly subjects that populate his life. While Carraway claims he wants "no more privileged glimpses into the human heart," his romantic view of Gatsby, his "unaffected scorn," shows he is unable to carry out his father's advice (4). Even Carraway admits that when it comes to conduct, he "doesn't care what it's founded on" (4). Because Gatsby's conduct is founded on his lifelong love for Daisy, the reader knows Gatsby cares deeply about what *his* conduct is founded on. Carraway's conduct, however, is founded on air, on privilege, and on selfishness. The very thing that "preyed on Gatsby" causes Carraway to lose interest in what he dismissively and condescendingly calls the "short-winded elations of men" (5).

Carraway is a cynic, and his seductive and detached narration invites the reader into the cynicism his privileges construct. Even his last name, Carraway, suggests that all of his empathy has been carried away and replaced with his advantaged perspective. It's as if he's saying to us: *Go ahead you silly humans. Hope and dream and fall in love, but when your hope dies and you're floating dead in a swimming pool, I'll be deep in the Midwest drinking gin.*

Thesis Paragraph Slant 1

Thesis Paragraph Slant 2

5: Constructing Body Paragraphs

Approach

1. Using the Outline

When writing a draft, there's a fine line between using the outline too much and not using it enough. If you don't use the outline enough, you run the risk of losing the structure and logic you've set for your essay. Why ditch it now?

On the other hand, using the outline too religiously can lead to a dry, fractured, and dead essay. Because fresh, flowing, conversational and dynamic writing is a part of your *Slant*, allowing yourself to get swept up in the continuity of your writing is just as important as using the logic of your outline.

Remind yourself to "check in" with your outline consistently, so you don't go off on too many tangents. The outline is your blueprint. The essay is your house. If you don't use the blueprint, your bathroom might end up in your kitchen or your house will fall apart. If you build what you designed in the blueprint, your house will be three dimensional, strong, and beautiful.

2. Writing Out of Order

Once you have your blueprint, you can begin construction. What you need are materials—doors, windows, wood, etc. These materials are your paragraphs. You can construct them in any order. Many successful writers write their essays out of order. In the end, with a little revision, the pieces will all fit together.

It really doesn't matter how you do it. Every writer is different. What matters is that you understand you don't have to write in order. Your paragraphs can move. Just because you write them in one place doesn't mean they have to stay there.

Rehearse

1. Topic Sentences

Okay, yes, it's a boring phrase. But without topic sentences in just the right places, your paragraphs are incoherent. Really, once you master topic sentences, you'll never know why you had a problem writing them. They're easy. They include two important things:

1. The topic of the paragraph.
2. Your *Slant* about the topic.

That's it. Sounds so simple, right? Though some writers think a topic sentence is always one sentence at the beginning of the paragraph, I like to think of it in the plural: topic sentences. Occasionally, one sentence will do it, but don't feel like you have to accomplish everything in one sentence. Let's take a look at the topic sentences at the beginning of one of Jennifer's paragraphs in "Being Innately Woman":

> Deer are typically docile creatures, especially to those more aggressive than them. But if the well-being of a doe's fawn is threatened, she will attack with no regard for her own welfare. The same concept applies to Clytaemnestra.

Here, in these three sentences, Jennifer establishes her topic: Clytaemnestra's aggression. She also conveys her *Slant*: Her aggression is defensive and as natural as a doe's.

Here are the topic sentences of one of Pablo's body paragraphs:

> While Nick Carraway is obviously the narrator of a novel and has the duty to bring the story to the reader, his own imagination often gets away from him. Because of his "advantage" in life, everything he assumes automatically becomes "true," as far as the reader is concerned.

Pablo is doing a lot in these two topic sentences. Not only does he state both the topic and his *Slant* about that topic, he also indicates the importance of a "challenge." Pablo's admission that Nick Carraway is narrating a fiction is an important way to acknowledge and control an opposition point.

Don't worry about a one-sentence topic sentence. Instead, remember the function of topic sentences and the logic of your paragraph. Most paragraphs convey their topic and their *Slant* in the first few sentences. That way, your following analysis will support it. If your topic sentence(s) is at the bottom of the paragraph, make sure it's there for a good reason.

2. Research on Demand

As you write your draft, pay attention to the holes that may pop up in your argument. Research is an ongoing process during drafting.

Arrange your research materials around your desk and computer so they're easily accessible as you write.

3. Paraphrasing

I know it's hard to resist those huge block quotes taken from a source that make your page count that much larger. But quit thinking like a writer, and start thinking like a reader. Unless that block quote is absolutely essential, we hate reading them. In fact, let's admit it, we don't. We skip them.

That's why we paraphrase. Paraphrasing is rewording a passage from a text in your own words. Let's review how Jennifer does it for her essay "Being Innately Woman." First, we'll take a look at the original passage she's using from Sophocles's "Antigone":

> You ought to realize we are only women,
> not meant in nature to fight against men,
> and that we are ruled, by those who are stronger,
> to obedience in this and even more painful matters.
> (Sophocles 163)

Here's Jennifer's paraphrase:

> You should know that, because we are just women, we're weak against the strength of men. They are born stronger. They rule us, and our role is to obey them and the laws they create, even when it's painful. (Sophocles 163)

Jennifer includes every idea from Sophocles. She is now ready to use the entire paraphrase, or just part of it, in her essay. Use only what you need—what supports your *Slant*.

Choose a key passage from the text or from your research and reword it now. Make sure your paraphrase is longer than the original. Dig deep. This method will save you time and help you think about the impact and meaning of the text.

4. Quote and Support Variation

There is nothing more boring than reading an essay that makes a point and then quotes the text over and over and over in the exact same way. The way you use your support should vary. There are many ways to use support from a text. They include block quotations, sentence quotations, partial quotations, paraphrases, and summaries. All of these tools need to be in your toolbox as a writer.

Block Quotation

A block quotation is a quote that's over four lines long and is indented in your essay. Here's an example, quoted from Richard A. Lanham's book called *Style: An Anti-Textbook*:

> Words are to use. Advertising, in supplying plastic soul to the media, literally *uses up* words for profit. It parodies divinity in turning the word into matter, into goods. Every day of his life, an American encounters the word primarily in someone's effort to sell him something. He must train himself to look through the word to the trap beneath. Enjoy the language and they've got you. Karl Shapiro called advertising the poetry of the poor. It is the poetry of us all—a poetry that travesties poetry, where the words never exist for themselves, where dignity, shape, form is never respected, where they are perpetually for sale. Advertising is America's real composition class, its real training in prose style. (Lanham 15)

Notice that in block quotations, because we indent them, we don't need quotation marks. However, avoid using block quotations unless there is a large portion of the text you absolutely must provide the reader word-for-word. How many of you just skipped over the block quotation above?

Sentence Quotation

This is the most common form of providing support in an essay. However, like the block quotation, sentence quotations should be used sparingly. If you can't say it better than the author, quote the entire sentence.

> "Advertising is America's real composition class, its real training in prose style" (Lanham 15).

Because sentence quotations are the most common, writer's often overuse them. Most of the time, you can say it better than the author of some other book or article said it. Choose your sentence quotations carefully. Below are three ways to vary it up.

Partial Quotation

A partial quote uses only a portion of the sentence from the text. For example, let's use Lanham's above sentence quotation and turn it into a partial quotation:

> Advertising is one of the last places in America that provides any real "training in prose style" (Lanham 15).

Paraphrase

We've been through paraphrasing earlier in *Slant*. That's because it's extremely important and deserves more attention than it gets. Here's an example paraphrase:

> **Quote:**
>
> "Advertising is America's real composition class, its real training in prose style" (Lanham 15).
>
> **Paraphrase:**
>
> If a writer is looking for a good place to learn about style, he or she should look to advertising (Lanham 15).

Summary

Summary seems like an easy idea, but it's often harder than writers suspect. Often, it may seem easier to just cut and paste block quotes or sentence quotations from a source. However, readers like to read *your* essay, *your* style, not someone else's.

Here's an example of a one sentence summary of Robert Lanham's block quotation paragraph above:

> Advertising exploits language into unsophisticated poetry, and has played a crucial role in many Americans' lack of skill and integrity when it comes to their writing styles (Lanham 15).

You'll notice that even though I didn't directly quote Lanham in either the paraphrase or the summary, I still cite the source. If I don't, it's stealing Lanham's ideas and presenting them as my own. That's plagiarism. If the idea comes from anywhere other than your own brain synapses, cite the source. No exceptions.

Create

1. SSS: *Slant*, Support, Synthesis

Nothing is more fun to read than a dynamic and well-structured paragraph—one that flows from the last and builds up to the next.

We've already talked about topic sentences. That's what usually comes first in a paragraph—*usually* because not all paragraphs are the same. Just because most paragraphs have a fundamental order and structure, doesn't mean all your paragraphs will adhere to it. Writing essays is art. As I stated earlier, before you can start experimenting, before you can start splattering paint on the canvas like Jackson Pollock, you have to master the fundamentals. The paragraph is a biggie. But don't be intimidated. It's a lot easier than you think, and it's based on a simple three-part structure: *Slant*, Support, Synthesis (SSS).

2. *Slant*

Start with your opinion and the topic. Make a claim. The first part of the paragraph should include a mini-thesis statement, or what we call the topic sentence(s). Use your outline. Your A's and B's and C's under numbers 3, 4, and 5... are focused on subpoints and details that prove your "supported bys" (which go on to prove your core *Slant*). Use them.

3. Support

After making a claim, you need to back it up with evidence. Support often comes in the form of analysis and research. In a research essay, support is made up of information you've gleaned from primary and secondary sources. Question: What's the difference? Answer:

Primary Sources: Research you've done
  - ➤ Observations
  - ➤ Interviews
  - ➤ Surveys
  - ➤ Experiments
  - ➤ Photographs
  - ➤ Artwork
  - ➤ Objects you've discovered (letters, art, journals…)
  - ➤ Literature

Secondary Sources: Research others have done
  - ➤ Nonfiction books that analyze information
  - ➤ Articles
  - ➤ Encyclopedias
  - ➤ Research reports

In a literary analysis essay about *The Great Gatsby*, for example, your support will come from *The Great Gatsby*—a primary source. However, if you decide to use a quote from a book of criticism about *The Great Gatsby*, that is a secondary source.

Use your Playlist for both primary and secondary sources. But don't depend solely on others' research. Personal observations, real-life examples, surveys or experiments you've conducted, interviews, even visuals are all valid primary sources. Support is like every other part of the writing process. It's creative. The best writers use support creatively, conjuring ingenious ways to support their *Slants*. If you approach an essay believing that support is merely quotations from texts, you're not writing an essay you would want to read. Like all aspects of your essay, you need variety. An adventure is no fun if you do the same thing every day, right? Likewise, an essay is no fun if you use the same texts over and over.

4. Synthesis

Synthesis is the explanation of how your support proves your topic sentence(s). For example, if you quote a text, make sure you both explain what the quote means and explain how it supports your point. Quotes don't always speak for themselves. Sure, to *you* the connection is clear, but a reader needs your explanation.

Pretend, for a moment, that you're a docent at a museum—one of those men or women who guide you through the exhibits and explain the art. They tell you about the history and context, but most importantly they offer up educated interpretations. When you're writing your paragraphs, you're the docent. You're the one who must guide, explain and interpret the support. Without you, the reader is lost deep in the maze of the museum.

4.5. A Note about Analysis

Analysis literally means "breaking up." Interestingly, synthesis and analysis are opposites. Synthesis means "bringing together." And yet, like many opposites, they're actually very similar when it comes to writing essays. Analysis is both about breaking things apart and about bringing them together to make new connections. For example, you might take some research or a passage from a text and look at details, breaking them up to examine the parts closely. You might then connect those details together and compare them. You're both breaking it up and connecting it together.

 In your essay, it is the combination of support and synthesis that makes up your analysis. Think of it like this: You have three gears in front of you. They are *Slant*, Support and Synthesis. When you put them together, they all rotate in unison and become analysis.

5. Sample SSS Paragraphs

Slant, Support and Synthesis work together in a paragraph to form a fluent unit. Let's take a look at a paragraph from Jennifer's essay, "Picking up the Heavy Nozzle—Scary, Right?":

Slant: Highlighted
Support: **Bold**
Synthesis: Underlined

> Gas station owners, however, have to protect their lives. In a post-9/11 culture intricately tangled with oil and terrorists, the American Dream is falling under siege in gas stations with the rise of hate crimes against immigrant owners and employees. While these immigrants came to pursue the American Dream of owning their own small business, such as gas stations and convenience stores, these very locations have become a hot spot for hate. According to Lisa Margonelli, author of the book *Oil on the Brain*, **"people who were angry at some vague combination of OPEC and Osama bin Laden attacked a hundred clerks at 7-Eleven gas stations and convenience stores in a month"** **(11)**. In addition, eight murders across the country directly following September 11, 2001 were linked to terrorist attack backlash. **Two murders on September 15 happened at a gas station and convenience store. The first victim, Balbir Singh Sodhi a "turban-wearing Sikh [was] killed outside his gas station" (Hanania) and the second, Waqar Hasan, a Pakistani, was shot to death in his convenience store.** Hate crimes escalated to phenomenal heights, with a **"1700 percent increase in the number of overall assaults and vandalism cases reported by Human Rights Watch during the first year after September 11th" (Hanania).** Immigrants once saw gas stations as an icon of prosperity; now they provide the setting for hate. No wonder people are afraid!

Notice how the second half of the paragraph is completely devoted to either support or synthesis. The first part of the paragraph is her *Slant*—her topic sentences. This paragraph perfectly forms the basic SSS structure, and uses a variety of techniques (sentence quotations, partial quotations, and paraphrasing) to provide support.

Let's take one more look at another paragraph from Jennifer's essay "Being Innately Woman."

Slant: Highlighted
Support: **Bold**
Synthesis: Underlined

In killing Agamemnon, Clytaemnestra's children, Orestes and Electra, and the public of Argos question her motives. They accuse her of being manipulative and power-hungry, calling her a controlling dictator. However, she states, **"And if I fall / the throne is yours,"** showing that having the crown is not her utmost priority **(1449-1450)**. Though Clytaemnestra realizes she will gain authority by murdering Agamemnon, she does not care much about keeping it. Power is a masculine desire, and only the men in her life, Agamemnon and Aegisthus, truly care about having it. Because Aegisthus is **"loyal to [her] as always,"** it is her womanly devotion to her lover, in addition to maternal instincts, that drives her to kill **(1463)**. Her motives behind the deed are completely female. She commits murder out of a need for love, while Aegisthus plans the murder out of a need for power.

Jennifer not only paraphrases and summarizes here, she explains, or synthesizes, her quotes for the reader. She does the work for **you** instead of making you do the work for her. By explaining her textual support, she makes her points clear and her argument persuasive.

Notice also how there is one sentence in the second half of the paragraph that isn't bolded or underlined. This sentence is a thesis reminder. It's a sentence that brings us back to the core argument, the Slant, of the essay to make sure that we understand how this paragraph and these ideas support her overall Slant (for more on writing thesis reminders, see the next chapter: Revising). Now, let's see how Pablo does it in his essay, "A Father's Advice: Advantage and Privilege in The Great Gatsby":

Slant: Highlighted
Support: **Bold**
Synthesis: Underlined

> While Nick Carraway is obviously the narrator of a novel and has the duty to bring the story to the reader, his own imagination often gets away from him. Because of his "advantage" in life, everything he assumes automatically becomes "true," as far as the reader is concerned. Before Carraway has ever met Gatsby, **he sees a figure emerge in the night from his "neighbor's mansion" (28).** Even though he has no idea what Gatsby looks like, Carraway immediately launches into assumptions. **He claims that the "leisurely movements" and the "secure position of his feet upon the lawn suggested that it was Gatsby himself" (28).** I don't know about you, but recognizing a man you have never met by the position of his feet on the lawn seems like a stretch. Nevertheless, Carraway doesn't stop there. He goes on to suggest that **Gatsby was out to "determine what share was his of our local heavens" (28).** Carraway projects his own advantage onto Gatsby. He is not only safe in his aloof and detached assumptions, he is right. To Carraway, the world is his oyster (or egg), and he has the luxury of deciding what share he's going to lay claim to. He lives a simple life in a small house in West Egg—that was his privileged choice. Gatsby, however, had to earn his choices.

Similar to Jennifer's paragraph, there's a one sentence thesis reminder in Pablo's body paragraph. He writes, "He is not only safe in his aloof and detached assumptions, he is right." Pablo does a great job of fluently combining *Slant*, support and synthesis.

6. Transitioning

In a perfect universe, you wouldn't need to transition—your ideas and language and paragraphs would flow like a beautiful river throughout your entire essay. In fact, only a small percentage of your paragraphs will need transition sentences. If every paragraph needs a transition, then you know there's something wrong with your essay. Most likely, you have too many separate ideas and topics, and you're not relating them to each other. You know how your paragraphs will logically and fluently flow into each other, but some of the time, you're going to have to make some connections for the reader.

A transition is always in the first sentence of a paragraph, not in the last sentence of a paragraph.

If you're having trouble thinking up a transition, first remember the word "connection." Your job is to connect one paragraph to another. The word transition doesn't help you much. Connection always reminds you what your duty is when writing a transition.

Try to avoid the cliché terms and phrases "also," "another," "in addition to," and "not only does..." These clunky terms and phrases are bush league attempts to connect paragraphs and ideas. Shoot for more elegant and subtle transitions.

Let's focus here on two important and elegant ways to connect two paragraphs:

1. Repeating words
2. Repeating structure

Yes, it's that easy. Often, the best way to transition is to do it with language not ideas. Let's look at a couple examples from Jennifer's essays.

Repeating words:

> ... The combination of these facts and warnings add to the expanding list of things to fear on the road. It isn't enough for Americans to protect their property at gas stations; we have to **protect** our credit scores too.
>
> Gas station owners, however, have to **protect** their lives. In a post-9/11 culture intricately tangled with oil and terrorists, the American Dream is falling under siege in gas stations with the rise of hate crimes against immigrant owners and employees.

Jennifer uses the word "**protect**" to transition from credit scores in paragraph one to protecting lives in paragraph two.

Repeating structure:

> ... Her flawed marriage makes it easier for Clytaemnestra to tap into the strength of her maternal instincts and view killing Agamemnon as a way to achieve justice. **By committing the crime**, she is speaking for the one who loved her: Iphigeneia.
>
> **By killing Agamemnon**, Clytaemnestra's children, Orestes and Electra, and the public of Argos question her motives. They accuse her of being manipulative and power-hungry, calling her a controlling dictator.

Take a look at the last sentence of the paragraph and the first sentence of the next paragraph. Is there a structure you can repeat? If not, could you create a structure to repeat?

Remember, these are not the only ways to transition. Sometimes you might be making such a big leap in ideas that you need a short transition paragraph to do the job. Other times, a repeated word or structure will mislead the reader and connect two ideas that have no connection. In those cases, you'll need to think about writing a full sentence that works as a transition.

6: Revising

Approach

1. Multiple Revisions

I know, the mere idea of revision strikes fear in your heart. You want to revise it once and be done with it. Trust me, I feel the same way when writing an essay. The problem is you cannot do everything in one revision. You have to break it up and focus on one or two features in each revision.

Here, we suggest a minimum of two revisions. That's not so bad, is it? The first revision is focused on structure and content. The second focuses on style and language.

Think of it like the process of building. Whether it's a house or a table or an artist's sculpture, you can't do the finishing work before you've properly prepared the framework, right? You can't put the finishing coat on a table top that hasn't yet been sanded.

You've already done the hard part. This is the fun part—when you get to see your essay come alive with ideas and style and fluency. You've already fried your doughnut. The revision is the glaze.

2. Writing Out Loud

Remember this from the Trifecta section? Well, this is another time when reading and writing out loud is crucial. You need to hear your own words on that page, so bark them out as you read through your essay. From this point on, **all the work is out loud**. No exceptions.

Read it to yourself. Read it to your roommate. Read it to your mom and dad. Read it to your instructor. Read it to the birds, okay? Better yet, let someone else read it back to you.

3. Writing for the Reader
Writing an Essay You Would Want to Read

Writing for the reader is probably the most overlooked point in student writing, especially in the revision process. Though your instructor grades your essay, your real audience is almost always your peers. Usually, instructors want to read your *Slant* through the perspective of the class as a continuation of class discussions, lectures, and class material.

You wrote your essay for you. You revise your essay for your audience. It's time to stop thinking of yourself as a writer now, and start thinking of yourself as a reader. You want your essay to be fun and interesting to read, right?

Since you've constructed the foundation of your essay, you need to test its logic. Your essay is not just a house. It's a home, so make it comfortable. The more of YOU you put into it, the more fun it's going to be. *Slant* isn't just your point of view; it's also the way you express yourself to the reader.

Rehearse

1. Only Connect: Writing Thesis Reminders

Sometimes, when we use the outline and work hard on the SSS of our paragraphs, our essays can appear to lose the connection to our core *Slant*. Because we've broken our essays into sub-points and topics, we have to make sure their connections to the *Slant* are still clear. A big part of writing for the reader is considering whether or not the readers are going to understand how your sub-points argue your main point—that's a connection you need to make for them if it is not already there.

Making that connection can often be as easy as revising your topic sentences so they include a connection to your *Slant,* or adding a sentence to the end of your paragraph. Remember Jennifer's thesis reminder in her paragraph from Constructing Body Paragraphs? Let's take a look. First, here is her thesis statement:

Although Clytaemnestra and Antigone, in their criminal pursuit of power and glory, act more like men than women,

their actions are driven by the female instincts of motherhood and sisterhood.

Now let's take a look at her thesis reminder in a body paragraph:

Thesis Reminder: <u>Underlined</u>

> In killing Agamemnon, Clytaemnestra's children, Orestes and Electra, and the public of Argos question her motives. They accuse her of being manipulative and power-hungry, calling her a controlling dictator. However, she states, "And if I fall / the throne is yours," showing that having the crown is not her utmost priority (1449-1450). Though Clytaemnestra realizes she will gain authority by murdering Agamemnon, she does not care much about keeping it. Power is a masculine desire, and only the men in her life, Agamemnon and Aegisthus, truly care about having it. Because Aegisthus is "loyal to [her] as always," it is her womanly devotion to her lover, in addition to maternal instincts, that drives her to kill (1463). <u>Her motives behind the deed are completely female.</u> She commits murder out of a need for love, while Aegisthus plans the murder out of a need for power.

Jennifer makes sure that the reader doesn't forget her *Slant*. She wants her paragraph to prove her thesis, right? So do you. A simple thesis reminder here and there can do wonders for the clarity and continuity of your core *Slant*.

Rewriting your *Slant* in different ways using different words will help both you and the reader understand it.

Create

1. The Reverse Outline

When I was an undergraduate, the mistake I often made when revising essays was to slog through it with no rhyme or reason, and certainly no plan. I'd read the essay through and make changes based simply on how things "sounded" in my head when I read them. I would read it several times, feel overwhelmed here and there, and continually fail to make the final, crucial changes that would turn that piece of writing from a draft into an essay.

If you're thinking right now, "Oh no, not another outline!" don't worry. The key to the reverse outline is keeping it simple. There's no complex format. The reverse outline is a straightforward step that will revolutionize the way you revise an essay. It's so easy that it seems like a shortcut. It seems that way because all of us have agonized over revisions in the past, wondering how to make this clearer or to make that more emphatic or connect this with that and where the heck did this idea come from and what the heck was I thinking putting this in and what am I going to do with it now—crap, I give up.

The reverse outline will make the process so logical and effective that you'll wonder why you haven't heard more about it. All you have to do is go through your essay and write a numbered list that contains the topic sentences or the core idea of each paragraph.

Let's look at Jennifer's reverse outline for her essay "Picking Up the Heavy Nozzle—Scary, Right?" Because Jennifer wrote a neutral opening, she starts with zero. If your opening is your opposition, start with one.

Picking Up the Heavy Nozzle—Scary, Right?
Reverse Outline

0. (Opening) On a hot summer afternoon when I was sixteen, filling up my car for the very first time, I officially became a small part of America's massive oil culture.

1. (Opposition) As Americans, <u>driving is our identity</u>.

2. (*Slant*) Gas stations embody the American culture of <u>crime and fear</u>.

3. The <u>media</u>'s obsession with gas station <u>crime</u> exaggerates its dangerous reputation.

4. Overexposure in the <u>media</u> has transformed gas stations' reputation past a mere hotspot for delinquent robbers. Gas stations are put in the <u>criminal spotlight</u>.

5. As if the gas station preoccupation of the news <u>media</u> were not already bad enough, <u>crime dramas</u> such as *CSI* and *Criminal Minds* often feature shady gas stations in their scripts.

6. Just when Americans thought a thief pretending to have a gun under his jacket was the worst thing that could happen to them at the pump, <u>advanced crimes</u> have found their way to gas stations, only adding to the aura of <u>paranoia</u>.

7. In a post-9/11 culture intricately tangled with oil and terrorists, the <u>American Dream</u> is falling under siege in gas stations with the rise of <u>hate crimes</u> against immigrant owners and employees.

8. Facts may support hate crimes at gas stations, but it's pure <u>fiction</u> that creates the lurking and <u>mysterious danger</u> at the pump.

9. In the land of <u>urban mythology</u>, gas stations are explosives waiting to blow up.

10. (Conclusion) Americans should know that gas stations are merely microcosms of a globe that is splattered and dripping in black oil, and our true fear is our inability to wipe away that oil stain smeared across this country's face.

Now, there are several things each writer needs to do when he or she finishes the reverse outline. First, read it over for logic and progression. I underlined the main ideas in each of Jennifer's sentences above. You'll notice that paragraphs 3, 4, and 5 all deal with the media, just like her first "supported by" in her original outline. Paragraphs 6 and 7 deal with gas station crime. Paragraph 8 builds off gas station crime and goes into the mythology of fear that surrounds gas stations because of that crime. Paragraph 9, then, expands on that idea of urban mythology. There's a clear and progressive logic there, right?

When I read Jennifer's reverse outline, I see several important clues. First, she has stuck pretty closely to her original outline. If you refer back to her original outline, however, you'll see that there are some points and some portions, some A's and B's, that she has left out. If that's the case with your essay, don't panic. For example, let's look at 3C from Jennifer's original outline:

C. Hedges eliminate escape routes for would-be robbers, and convenience store gas stations purchase "target hardening kits."

Jennifer never mentions anything about hedges being escape routes in her essay. She made the decision in her writing process that she didn't need that piece of information. It wasn't important enough to include. What you need to do now is compare your reverse outline with your original outline and decide if you need to add some ideas or paragraphs that you failed to incorporate from your original outline. While it's okay to let some points drop, make sure it's for a good reason.

The second thing I notice about Jennifer's reverse outline is that it gets problematically broad toward the end of the essay. Let's look at paragraphs 8 and 9:

> 8. Facts may support hate crimes at gas stations, but it's pure fiction that creates the lurking and mysterious danger at the pump.
>
> 9. In the land of urban mythology, gas stations are explosives waiting to blow up.

It's an effective technique to start very specific in your essay and then begin to broaden out a bit toward the end. That's the logic of Crescendo Analysis. However, one can lose control and broaden out too much. I would revise paragraphs 8 and 9 based on this reverse outline. Terms like "mythology," "pure fiction," "lurking," and "mysterious," while they attract attention, seem speculative and vague to me. I would focus these paragraphs on more specific points about the mythology. I might do a survey and go out and ask my peers what ideas come to mind when I say, "gas station." This might bring attention to some of the specific myths, and give me some ideas about how I might focus that portion of my essay on more concrete details and information.

Consider these questions when analyzing your reverse outline:

1. Why does my reverse outline differ from my original outline and are those changes effective?
2. Is there a progressive logic in the paragraphs? Do they build off one another, or would it be better to rearrange the order of my paragraphs?
3. Does each paragraph support some part of my *Slant*?
4. Do any paragraphs and/or sequence of paragraphs sound too general or vague? Do any seem off topic and difficult to connect with the *Slant*?
5. Are the statements in my reverse outline pointed and well-written? Are they topic sentences?
6. Does each paragraph have one core idea or do some paragraphs need to be broken up into more than one?

Based on your answers to these questions, begin the revision of your essay. If you need to add portions from your original outline that you failed to incorporate, start now. If your essay fails to contain a logical and fluent flow of information, start rearranging and revising paragraphs. If some of your paragraphs are broad or vague, revise them with more specific information and precision. If your paragraphs fail to connect to or support your *Slant*, you either need to revise them so that the connection is clear and effective or cut them out completely. As writers, sometimes we go on tangents that lead us down dead end avenues. If that's one of your problems, it should be clear in the reverse outline.

When you have appraised your essay based on your reverse outline, use the below techniques to revise the structure and content.

2. First Revision Based on Reverse Outline: Structure and Content

Jujitsu and Dynamite:

Pretend now that you're a trained jujitsu master and a certified and licensed detonator of dynamite. The first thing to do when starting revision is to clench your fists and light the match. Attack every paragraph with mad fighting and explosive skills—kicking portions of paragraphs around and exploding long and dense paragraphs into multiple paragraphs. Here, you'll use the information you gleaned in your analysis of your reverse outline to attack paragraphs straight on.

Jujitsu: Come on, get mean. Think of every paragraph as a group of opponents. Think of your entire essay as an angry army. Time to go on the offensive and do some damage. Kick transition sentences from the last sentence of a paragraph to the beginning of the next. Throw topic sentences to the place they belong. Based on your reverse outline kick paragraphs around and see if they fit better somewhere else.

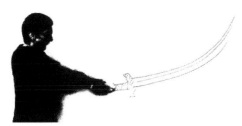 Many writers, because they're thinking the most clearly at the end of their essay, find that their conclusion or last paragraph is actually their thesis paragraph. That's great. Now just jujitsu your conclusion into the thesis paragraph slot in the Trifecta of your essay.

The same goes for sentences in paragraphs. Follow the SSS method of constructing paragraphs and start kicking them into shape.

Dynamite: If you have paragraphs that are a page long or more, cram a stick of dynamite inside them. Break them up. If you have portions in your reverse outline that seem too broad and vague, blow them up and make them more specific. If you have paragraphs that are all the same length, put a stick of dynamite in your entire essay. Writing a dynamic essay demands variety—sentence and paragraph variety. Now's the time to shorten up those rambling paragraphs. We use the term "dynamic" for a reason.

Structure and Content:

As you're using jujitsu and dynamite to rearrange and explode your paragraphs, don't forget to keep the entirety in mind. When you're reading and revising for structure and content, ask these questions:

Attacking Structure:

1. Does your Trifecta work as a unit, hooking the reader and clarifying your *Slant*?
2. Are your paragraphs in a logical order, and is there a progression of thought in your essay?
3. Does your thesis paragraph fully explain and set up your *Slant*? How can you revise it to make it stronger?

Attacking Content:

1. Are there holes in your argument?
2. Is there any additional research, examples or analysis that would help support and clarify your points?
3. Do you have transitions and thesis reminders?

Read it out loud. **Louder.** Take revision notes as you go.

3. Second Revision: Style and Language

After you've completed your revision based on your reverse outline and you have what you consider a logical and complete essay, leave your original outline and reverse outline behind. They're history now. They've served their purpose. Now it's time to focus on the flow of your sentences.

The last revision is proofreading. You want to read your essay for errors and style. The style of the essay is the sound and rhythm of your sentences. Peer tutors, editors, and friends are often best at making comments about style and language. Reading your essay out loud to someone else will actually help you hear it too.

If you've read your own essay on your computer screen over and over, print it out now and read it in hardcopy. When you're doing your final revision, it's best to try and forget you wrote it. Pretend it is someone else's essay. Reading a hardcopy can help distance you a bit. Waiting a couple hours and returning to your work later helps too.

Mark the hardcopy up with a pen or pencil, circling errors, omitting needless words and phrases, and revising sentences that sound awkward. Here are five questions to ask while you read:

1. Is there a simpler, more dynamic way to say this?
2. Are my sentences varied in length and structure?
3. Is this essay free of typos and grammatical errors?
4. Have I used and cited sources correctly, and have I constructed a Works Cited page?
5. Is my writing engaging? Do you get a sense of the author from the writing style?

There are two primary types of stylists out there: painters and sculptors. Painters keep adding paint to their canvases. Sculptors hack away chunks and bits from marble or clay or wood. The same applies for writers in revision. Some writers, when they reach this last stage, need to paint the picture. They need to add explanation and language and color and variety. Other writers, the sculptors, need to cut repetitive, wordy, and turgid parts away. If you need help, do yourself a favor and ask someone to read your essay. Get some feedback. You might even ask a friend to read your essay out loud to you. It can often be very revealing to hear your own words.

4. Peer Review

Many of you may have tried handing off your essays to your friends or your older sisters or even a tutor. That's a great idea. However, even though their feedback is well intentioned, sometimes you need more detailed and focused criticism.

While those people may have the skills it takes to give you quality feedback, they don't have specific and logical questions in front of them to answer—questions about the success of specific parts of your essay. They need a form.

What follows is a peer review form. Very often, having good readers read your essay and answer these questions can be the most beneficial revision strategy, and I highly encourage every writer to use this peer review form to get feedback.

Essay Peer Review

Your Name:_____Writer's Name:_____

1. How does the title of the essay affect you as a reader?

2. Locate the thesis paragraph(s). How can the thesis paragraph (usually NOT the first paragraph) be stronger and clearer? Is the writer convincing there? What would you suggest be added to make it clearer and more emphatic?

3. Can you locate a paragraph of opposing argument? Does the opposing argument offer examples? How can the writer more successfully use an alternative viewpoint to clarify his or her *Slant* or thesis?

4. How effective is the opening paragraph in engaging and interesting you as a reader, and how can it be improved?

(over)

Peer Review (Back)

5. Which body paragraphs need improvement? What are they lacking? Are they lacking support? Explanation from the writer? Examples? Be specific.

6. How can the writer be more effective? Are there stylistic ways the writer can make the essay more enjoyable to read?

7. How can the conclusion provoke ideas *beyond* the thesis? Does the conclusion give you a sense of some larger implications of the essay, and add something *new* to your understanding?

8. Your overall suggestions (Be specific, and avoid "like," "dislike," "good," "bad"):

(Download Peer Review assignment sheet at www.NicholasLeither.com)

7: Writing the Conclusion

Approach

1. Forgetting Everything You Ever Learned About Conclusions

Remember how some teacher or student or textbook once told you to restate your thesis in your conclusion? Forget it. If you've written a great essay that explores and argues your *Slant* properly, repeating it is only, well, repetitive.

Did someone tell you to sum up your essay in the conclusion? Forget it.

Did they tell you that the conclusion finishes the analysis and argument of the essay's body? Forget it. You've already done all that. It's time to do something wild and different.

The key word to keep in mind in the concluding paragraph is this: **Provocation**.

2. Provocation

 We all like provocative endings, and there are thousands of ways to provoke your readers. What about your essay provokes you? What makes you think? What makes you react? If you were the reader, what part of your essay would make you want to participate in the *Slant*?

Go back to the topic generating stage of this essay and ask yourself what provoked you the most when you first started thinking, writing, and researching this topic. Those initial provocations may lead you to the topic of your conclusion.

Don't forget to think about the reader. Think of your conclusion like the end of a good book or even a movie. The best endings are the ones that leave you thinking and wanting more, right? So leave your readers with something new to ponder.

Rehearse

1. Writing the Next Essay

You've just written an engaging essay with a strong *Slant*. It's so focused and specific that you want to give your readers a sense of the bigger picture. The best way to think about that bigger picture is to ask this question:

> If I were going to write another, bigger essay (or even a book) building off this essay, what would that essay be about?

The answer to that question can provide the topic for your conclusion. See the Create section of this chapter for Jennifer's example.

2. So What?

Have you ever read an interesting essay that left you wanting to know what it was really about and why it was important to read? That's an example of a writer who hasn't provided the "So what?" That writer hasn't expressed the significance of his or her essay.

The conclusion helps make those essential connections for the reader. Think of your essay as a classroom and think of yourself as the teacher. In the classroom you teach your students the necessary book knowledge, but before they head out into the world you have to make it clear how they can use that book knowledge in the real world, right? It's the same thing with your conclusion. If the connection between the essay and life isn't clear, it's time to make it clear.

Create

1. Evoking Curiosity

You can't ask for a better reader than one who's curious about your topic. But you can't ask for a better writer than one who makes you curious about a topic you weren't curious about in the first place.

We all like being left with a sense that we learned something, that the writer engaged us, and left us wondering and thinking. When you first lay your fingers on the keyboard to start writing your conclusion, try to answer these questions:

1. Why did you choose this topic in the first place?
2. What about this topic piqued your curiosity?
3. What is the single most fascinating thing you discovered about your topic and *Slant* along the way?
4. If you were reading this essay, what would fascinate you the most?
5. What is the most interesting connection you've made from your *Slant* to the bigger picture?

These questions will lead you to details that belong in your conclusion. Remember, you don't have to say it all in your conclusion. You just want to leave the reader with something to ponder.

Let's take a look at Jennifer's conclusion from her essay, "Being Innately Woman." Notice how she uses her *Slant* to transition into the bigger picture, and leaves the reader with an idea about modern politics to ponder.

Though killing a husband and burying a brother are clearly different things, both deeds require the kind of emotional potency only a woman can muster. The acts of these women require strength and commitment; however, their emotional endurance enables them to tolerate the pain that comes with losing loved ones and preserving their memory. Unlike men, they are heart-strong instead of headstrong. Their deeds are driven by the heart, by love, and by devotion, not by greed or glory. Often, leaders are accused of being heartless, insensitive, and selfish. Often, these leaders are men. Yet, a tremendous fear of women in power prevails, even in modern-day politics. Perhaps civilized cultures have an inherent desire to keep women in their place, confined to power only in the domestic setting. But taking into consideration the power of female emotional strength, like Clytaemnestra's and Antigone's, women leaders may provide a refreshing alternative to traditional roles of power. The question now is whether the public is ready to be ruled by the heart-strong leadership of women.

2. The Solution

If you wrote a cause-and-effect essay, or an essay about a problem, the conclusion can often be the solution or a series of solutions. For example, if you wrote an essay arguing that skimpy clothing ads and styles cause teen promiscuity, your conclusion might suggest that clothing companies have a responsibility to the public. It might be that clothing companies should have stricter restrictions on how they advertise and market clothing to teens. It might be that consumers have to be more aware and wise about the trends that clothing companies promote and the reasons they promote them.

With the solution, as with any conclusion, you have to consider the reader. Because the reader of the clothing essay is more likely to be a consumer, it might be better to gear the conclusion toward the consumer. What can the average consumer do to solve the problem? Remember, writing isn't always about making the choice that seems the strongest. It's often about making the choice that is most geared to the audience.

Let's take a look at Lydia's conclusion from "Quitting Cold Turkey."

> Thanksgiving is certainly not the only place where social norms create difficult moral dilemmas. Injustice is everywhere. It permeates our families, communities, and the world. So many of us turn a blind eye. Yet, there are some who fight for justice, who change their minds, hearts and actions to fight those things that oppose their values. It's always easier to say, "Someone else will fight this" or "My contribution cannot possibly make a difference," but that is exactly the type of thinking that allows for injustice and blocks positive change. Each choice to change has a ripple effect. It is crucial, and, yes, it is difficult. It is a heavy burden to put into action the part of your heart that wants to "save the world." But if not my family and me, then who?

Here, she provokes the reader, connects her family's Thanksgiving choices to our tendency to overlook larger injustices, and manages to point a finger at the reader by pointing a finger at herself and her family. The solution she suggests here is for all of us to be aware of our choices and stop ignoring injustices.

3. Slant

You are now a Slant pro, and it's in the conclusion where being a Slant pro pays off. The last paragraph of your essay should be overflowing with YOU. Get your attitude in there. Get your personality in there. Get your own words in there. Leave the reader with an idea of the kind of person who wrote it. Get your enthusiasm in there too. After all, you want the reader to feel like he or she is part of the adventure. That adventure doesn't end when your essay ends. Hopefully, your readers will want to start an adventure all their own. Effective conclusions are not endings, but new beginnings.

8: Sample Essays

This chapter contains Jennifer Tang's two essay projects and Lydia Davidson's essay project.

Sample Essay Project 1

Being Innately Woman:
The Characters of Clytaemnestra and Antigone
By Jennifer Tang

In Greek mythology, Helen, Penelope, and Jocasta represent the objects over which men fight wars, the loyal wives to whom brave warriors return, and unknowing,

> **Trifecta:** Opening Paragraph (Chapter 4)

helpless wives and mothers. Throughout Greek texts like the *Odyssey* and "Oedipus the King," women are portrayed traditionally—as vulnerable, as conformists, and as dependent. Characterized as idle creatures, Greek women often commit their loyalty and submit their freewill to the likes of men. According to the character Ismene in Sophocles' "Antigone" women are "not meant in nature to fight against men, / and [they] are ruled, by those who are stronger" ("Antigone" *lines* 71-72). However, two women defy these female norms. Clytaemnestra and Antigone challenge the limitations of their gender and become models for modern-day feminism. They refuse to conform to the conventional roles of women in Greek mythology, but does this make them any less womanly?

Much of Clytaemnestra's and Antigone's strengths are credited to the notion that they have masculine personalities. Clytaemnestra speaks "like a man ... full of self-command" ("Agamemnon" *lines* 355-356). Even Creon, the king in "Antigone," suspects a "man who with his own hand did the [illegal] burial" when Antigone, a young woman, proves to be the culprit ("Antigone" 337-338). Because they do what typical women cannot or refuse to do, readers often perceive Clytaemnestra and Antigone as less womanly. Readers rationalize their deviant behavior by believing that Clytaemnestra and Antigone are motivated by their unorthodox, masculine personalities. For instance, the Watchman says about Clytaemnestra, "So she commands, full of her high hopes. / That woman—she manoeuvres like a man" ("Agamemnon" 12-13). And Antigone refuses to take her sister's advice when she fights against men, despite it being against a woman's nature ("Antigone" 71). A greed for power and a lust for glory spur men to commit their crimes. Therefore, Clytaemnestra and Antigone are out of tune with

> Trifecta:
> Opposition
> Paragraph
> (Chapter 4)

the female norms of compassion and loyalty that define other women in Greek mythology, like Penelope.

However, Clytaemnestra and Antigone, though

| Trifecta: |
| Thesis/Slant |
| Paragraph |
| (Chapter 4) |

untraditional, bolder, and more radical, are no less compassionate, loyal, or loving than other women in Greek mythology. They are not men, nor are they trying to be like men; rather it is the very core of their womanhood that leads them to commit their crimes. Maternal and sisterly instincts drive Clytaemnestra and Antigone to aggressive actions. After all, a mere man like Aegisthus would not have murdered a war hero just to avenge the death of a daughter. A young man like Haemon would not have defied the king simply to fulfill a divine family duty. Clytaemnestra does not murder her husband, Agamemnon, because of a masculine greed for power. No, she murders her husband because of female grief and a desire for vengeance on behalf of her murdered daughter. Antigone does not bury her brother because of a boyish rebellious nature or a hunger for glory. No, she rebels in order to fulfill her divine duty as a sister and to pay respect to a beloved, fallen brother. Neither woman deserves to be accused for taking on roles unnatural to them. Instead,

Clytaemnestra and Antigone deserve to be celebrated for embracing their primal, womanly instincts and obligations fully, even if it means personal doom.

Maternal instincts are among the most innate of natural impulses, as well as one of the most primal. For example, deer are typically docile creatures, especially to those more aggressive than them. But if the well-being of a doe's fawn is threatened, she will attack with no regard for her own welfare. The same concept applies to Clytaemnestra. Mothers will do all they can to protect their children, and when they cannot, feeling a sense of failure is unavoidable. This is the catalyst behind Clytemnestra's actions. She describes her daughter Iphigeneia as "the agony I laboured into love," signifying the level of intimacy between a mother and a daughter, the result of arduous childbirth ("Agamemnon" 1443). The bond between a mother and her daughter drove her to commit the bloody deed. Clytaemnestra may seem cold and callous in "Agamemnon," but, like the doe, she is willing to do anything necessary to protect her daughter. When she fails to protect her, she has no other choice but to take revenge on Agamemnon, who

Jennifer's repetition of "primal" creates a transition. (Chapter 5)

Jennifer returns to the doe, strengthening the analogy

"thought no more of [sacrificing Iphigenia] than killing a beast" (1440).

When Clytaemnestra is misunderstood as cold-hearted, the womanly motivation that drove her to murder is often forgotten. Aeschylus only tells the story of Agamemnon's death; as readers we do not know Clytaemnestra's character before Agamemnon sacrifices their daughter. Clytaemnestra describes Agamemnon as one of these "deadly men / who seem to love you" (1393-1394) and blames him for flooding "the vessel of our proud house with misery" (1421). Although both spouses have extramarital affairs, their mutual unfaithfulness shows that Clytaemnestra and Agamemnon's union is flawed. Her husband's indifference may have driven her to latch onto her child's love. After Agamemnon takes her daughter away, Cltytaemnestra says, "he brutalized me" (1464). Her flawed marriage makes it easier for Clytaemnestra to tap into the strength of her maternal instincts and view killing Agamemnon as a way to achieve justice. By committing the crime, she is speaking for the one who loved her: Iphigeneia.

152

By killing Agamemnon, Clytaemnestra's children,

Orestes and Electra, and the public of Argos, question her

motives. They accuse her of being manipulative and power-

hungry, calling her a controlling dictator. However, she states,

"And if I fall / the throne is yours," showing that having the

crown is not her utmost priority (1449-1450). Though

Clytaemnestra realizes she will gain authority by murdering

Agamemnon, she does not care much about keeping it.

Power is a masculine desire, and only the men in her life,

Agamemnon and Aegisthus, truly care about having it.

Because Aegisthus is "loyal to [her] as always," it is her

womanly devotion to her lover, in addition to maternal

instincts, that drives her to kill (1463). Her motives behind the

deed are completely female. She commits murder out of a

need for love, while Aegisthus plans the murder out of a need

for power.

Antigone's reasons for her crime are not much

different from that of Clytaemnestra. Again, a familial tie

motivates her to defy the king's law. In fact, Antigone does

not see burying her brother Polyneices as defiance at all.

Rather she says, "It is not for [Creon] to keep me from my

> Jennifer uses a repeating structure as a transition (Chapter 5)

> This sentence is a thesis reminder, bringing the reader back to Jennifer's core Slant (Chapter 6).

own" ("Antigone" 54). As a woman in the family, her sisterly responsibility demands that Polyneices receive a proper burial, which outweighs her civic responsibility to follow the law. To her, nothing else matters, not even her life. She tells Ismeme, "Life was your choice, and death was mine" (610). Antigone's devotion to another person and her selflessness grows out of her innate womanly instinct to care for loved ones. Just like the doe that places her life in danger, Antigone is willing to jeopardize herself for a family member.

> Repeating a previous analogy brings continuity to the essay.

　　　　Many men in Greek mythology, on the other hand, jeopardize their integrity for personal gain. To them, it is simply a game to win or lose. Creon explains, "we cannot give victory to a woman … we must not let people say that a woman beat us" (732, 734). He cares only about his reputation with the people of Thebes. Conversely, Antigone has no intention of winning or losing. Her sole concern is doing the right thing. "I know I am pleasing those I should please most" and those people are her family, her brothers, the ones divine law deems most important (103). Unlike Creon, Antigone realizes that her family is more important than the public. Her priorities are straight and her intentions

> Jennifer's repetition of "jeopardize" creates a transition (Chapter 5).

are selfless. Though "the city mourns for this girl" and sides

with her, she cares little about public opinion (747). Creon,

however, bases his decisions on power and greed. Creon's

masculine desire for power highlights Antigone's female

virtue, demonstrating the stark contrast between their

motivations.

Though killing a husband and burying a brother are

clearly different things, both deeds require the kind of

emotional potency only a woman can muster. The acts of

these women require strength and commitment; however,

their emotional endurance enables them to tolerate the pain

that comes with losing loved ones and preserving their

memory. Unlike men, they are heart-strong instead of

headstrong. Their deeds are driven by the heart, by love, and

by devotion, not by greed or glory. Often, leaders are accused

of being heartless, insensitive, and selfish. Often, these

leaders are men. Yet, a tremendous fear of women in power

prevails, even in modern-day politics. Perhaps civilized

cultures have an inherent desire to keep women in their

place, confined to power only in the domestic setting. But

taking into consideration the power of female emotional

Conclusion: Jennifer focuses on the bigger picture and the "so what?" to conclude her essay (Chapter 7).

strength, like Clytaemnestra's and Antigone's, women leaders may provide a refreshing alternative to traditional roles of power. The question now is whether the public is ready to be ruled by the heart-strong leadership of women.

Works Cited

Aeschylus. *The Oresteia*. Trans. Robert Fagles. New York: Penguin Books, 1977. Print.

Sophocles. Trans. David Grene. *Sophocles I*. Chicago: The University of Chicago Press, 1991. Print.

Sample Essay Project 2

Picking Up the Heavy Nozzle—Scary, Right?
By Jennifer Tang

I was only sixteen and it was my very first time. Though I had come to this place a thousand times before, I was scared and unsure whether I knew how to do it right. I was now going to fill up a gas tank by myself. Steven, my driving instructor, had already taught me how to weave through thick downtown traffic and maneuver steep hills, but going to the gas station made me uneasy. We pulled up to a Chevron in a neighborhood full of pastel-colored homes and family-owned restaurants; it was shiny, clean, and the sun glistened off the sharp steel edges of the gas pump. As I nervously picked up the heavy nozzle, Steven explained in his broken English the steps to "fill 'er up": Hand the clerk two $20 bills, place the nozzle in the car, lift the handle, push the button, and watch the digital numbers stir. The process was very mechanical. Before I knew it, Steven's double-pedaled Corolla was ready to go. I took a sip of my Coke from the

> **Trifecta:**
> Opening Paragraph (Chapter 4).
>
> Jennifer uses a personal anecdote to open her essay.
>
> Details and descriptive language enliven her writing (Chapter 6).

convenience store, feeling extremely relieved, but I didn't

know why. That hot summer afternoon was the day I officially

became a small part of America's massive oil culture.

Like taking the SATs or going to the prom, filling up at

the gas station for the first time has become a milestone for

every American teenager. Part of the United States' identity is

rooted in the ideal that every American can own a car—a

revolution sparked by Henry Ford's Model T. For many

Trifecta: Opposition Paragraph (Chapter 4)

Americans, driving their cars is an inherent part of everyday

life. Going to the gas station is equivalent to the French

running to the bakery for a baguette. Driving is our identity.

Accelerating on an open highway captures American freedom

in its truest form and "studies show that people love being

alone in their cars more than, say, being at work or at home"

(Margonelli 32). Gas stations act as pseudo concierge services

that offer winning lottery tickets and an endless variety of

soft drinks and snacks to maximize the driving experience.

Other nations have monarchies, monuments, and museums

to represent their country. Americans have cars. Gas stations

are the backbone of America's rich and prosperous identity—

158

the castles full of liquid gold and black jewels that keep our

nation running.

On the surface, gas stations are ordinary places of

consumption in our capitalist country. Underneath their shiny

exteriors, they **embody the American culture of crime and

fear.** What many overlook are gas stations' hidden evils.

Chevron, Shell, and the local independent station are all

microcosmic melting pots of America, where wealthy and

poor, model citizens and thieves, come together.

Except we don't really think about this.

These ordinary businesses on intersections and

freeway exits are America's poster-children for fright. This

explains why I felt anxious that day at Chevron with Steven,

or why many of my friends' fathers insist on going to the gas

station for them. In the media, evening broadcasts and

newspaper articles report gas station crimes repeatedly, and

just about every primetime crime drama films scenes by the

pump. As a result, the media helps establish gas stations as a

bustling crime center, leading to urban myths about car

explosions and internet hoaxes about hidden needles. This

reputation creates a breeding ground for paranoia, where

> **Trifecta:
> Thesis Paragraphs**
> (Chapter 4)
>
> Jennifer splits her thesis paragraph into three with a short, stylistic sentence to keep the reader's attention (Chapter 6).
>
> Note how she returns to her personal anecdote here in her last thesis paragraph.

Americans fear lurking possibilities beyond robbery, such as identity theft and hate crimes. With so many possibilities, gas stations may seem almost as dangerous as the war zones where our soldiers fight to fill our pumps.

The media's obsession with gas station crime

> Strong, pointed topic sentence (Chapter 5).

exaggerates its dangerous reputation. In reality, gas stations are objects for robbery for just two reasons. Compared to other places one would consider robbing, such as a bank, the risks of robbing a gas station are much lower, lacking trained security guards, teller panic buttons, and hostage situations. Also, "[gas stations'] unique setting allows thieves to catch their victims by complete surprise" (Gas Station).

But overexposure in the media has transformed gas stations' reputation past a mere hotspot for delinquent robbers. Gas stations are put in the criminal spotlight. News reports portray them as prime targets for robbers. In reality, gas station robberies don't occur as often as we think, and in 2004 they actually decreased by 7.4 percent (Robbery). Still everybody from the news anchor to my father warns me to hang onto my wallet for dear life when filling 'er up. What is

> Jennifer uses common, informal language selectively to connect with the reader.

the cause of all this fear? According to the National Crime

Prevention Council, "there has been increased media coverage across the country regarding theft at gas stations" (Gas Station). The news media is primarily focused on gas station robbery—very few stories are published and broadcasted about the whopping 42.8 percent of robberies that occur on the street (Robbery). In contrast, almost all nine percent of gas station robberies are not only reported, but followed dutifully by the news media. Perhaps this is because the grainy images from gas station surveillance cameras add excitement to news broadcasts. Certainly an armed masked man taking some *Corn Nuts* with his sack of cash is an intriguing image, sure to raise television ratings and intrigue viewers. Why not show more of it? If something happens at a gas station, anyone who watches television is sure going to hear about it. The same happens in newspapers. In my research, I found three separate articles published within a span of two days in *The Philadelphia Inquirer* about a single gas station robbery. If Philadelphians didn't catch the first article about the robbery, they were bound to read the next two.

Jennifer is using research and support creatively here. Instead of using and quoting a source, she relays the results of her research in order to prove, through an example, that gas station robberies are often given unnecessary attention.

As if the gas station preoccupation of the news media were not already bad enough, crime dramas such as CSI and Criminal Minds often feature shady gas stations in their scripts. The most memorable scene from season three of Criminal Minds is when a serial killer stakes out a gas station for his next victim—a young brunette who comes out of the convenience store with a jug of milk. She heads for her car, and he effortlessly grabs her in broad daylight. Scenes like these suggest to television-watching Americans that the gas station serves as the criminal headquarters for all the bad apples in the world.

> She's making a creative argument, using information she created in her "Blowing Bubbles" exercise (Chapter 1).

Just when Americans thought a thief pretending to have a gun under his jacket was the worst thing that could happen to them at the pump, advanced crimes have found their way to gas stations, only adding to the aura of paranoia. In recent years, increasingly outlandish criminals strike at gas stations, committing identity theft and hate crimes. Technology analysts warn Americans that "using a credit card at a gas station could pose more of a risk for data theft than shopping online" (Kirk). Many gas station point-of-sale terminals (the machines through which we swipe our credit

> Strong and pointed topic sentence (Chapter 5).

cards) are connected to the Internet instead of dial-up networks to transmit data; therefore, "hackers lurk in parking lots looking for weak networks to penetrate" (Kirk). The statistics are staggering. As many as ten million Americans fall victim to identity theft a year (Identity). The combination of these facts and warnings add to the expanding list of things to fear on the road. It isn't enough for Americans to protect their property at gas stations; we have to protect our credit scores too.

Gas station owners, however, have to protect their lives. In a post-9/11 culture intricately tangled with oil and terrorists, the American Dream is falling under siege in gas stations with the rise of hate crimes against immigrant owners and employees. While these immigrants came to pursue the American Dream of owning their own small business, such as gas stations and convenience stores, these very locations have become a hot spot for hate. According to Lisa Margonelli, author of the book *Oil on the Brain*, "people who were angry at some vague combination of OPEC and Osama bin Laden attacked a hundred clerks at 7-Eleven gas stations and convenience stores in a month" (11). In addition,

Jennifer repeats the word "protect" as a transition (Chapter 5).

Introducing sources using synthesis (Chapter 5).

eight murders across the country directly following

September 11, 2001 were linked to terrorist attack backlash.

Two murders on September 15 happened at a gas station and

convenience store. The first victim, Balbir Singh Sodhi, a

"turban-wearing Sikh [was] killed outside his gas station"

(Hanania) and the second, Waqar Hasan, a Pakistani, was shot

to death in his convenience store. Hate crimes escalated to

phenomenal heights, with a "1700 percent increase in the

number of overall assaults and vandalism cases reported by

Human Rights Watch during the first year after September

11th" (Hanania). Immigrants once saw gas stations as icons of

prosperity; now they provide the setting for hate. No wonder

people are afraid!

    Facts may support hate crimes at gas stations, but it's

pure fiction that creates the lurking and mysterious danger at

the pump. As if Americans didn't already have enough to fear

at the pump, rumors and urban myths about explosions and

dirty needles creep into our minds while we gas up our cars.

Of these urban legends, the most outlandish is the HIV-

infected needles hidden under gas pump handles. This myth

was spread across the country via email, in which a fictional

Captain Abraham Sands writes, "In the Jacksonville area alone there have been seventeen cases of people being stuck by these needles over the past five months. We have verified reports of at least 12 others in various states around the country..." (Gasoline Myths). The email was a con. Such needles never existed, but its extensive circulation says a lot about Americans' willingness to buy into gas-station fear. Not only do we exaggerate the smallest fragments of danger, we fabricate all sorts of threats. Back in the 1990s, people were scared about infected needles in pay phone coin returns. Gas stations are now the new host of this mythology.

> Jennifer varies her sentences to create a dynamic essay. This short sentence breaks up the longer sentences that surround it (Chapter 6).

> Jennifer repeats the word "mythology" as a transition (chapter 5).

In the land of urban mythology, gas stations are explosives waiting to blow up. Combine two normal activities, such as filling the gas tank and talking on a cell phone, and beware! The chance of an explosion has risen exponentially. Similar to the needle legend, this rumor exploded on the Internet at the turn of the millennium and there are no reports of it actually happening. Both the cell phone and oil industries agree:

> The Cellular Telecommunications Industry Association has said, "There is no evidence whatsoever that a

wireless phone has ever caused ignition or explosion at a station anywhere in the world. Wireless phones don't cause gas stations to blow up." The American Petroleum Institute notes, "We can find no evidence of someone using a cell phone causing any kind of accident, no matter how small, at a gas station anywhere in the world. (Gasoline Myths)

Some drivers, unaware of the truth, cautiously inspect pump handles or nervously shut off their cell phones. Although these myths hold no shred of truth, they are so widely spread and commonly accepted that anyone exposed to pop culture is aware of them, even non-drivers, including yours truly. Myths about sea creatures or crop circles made people nervous at lakes and in the country. Now, the mysterious monsters hide behind gas pumps.

Despite Americans' fear, we continue to go to gas stations because we need oil to function. Our government, similarly, continues to sway diplomacy, impose sanctions, and fight wars in order to maintain this vicious cycle of need and fear. These antagonistic ways of obtaining oil permeate through the pipelines, coming out of gas station pumps in the

Jennifer uses herself throughout the essay to both support her *Slant* and connect with the reader.

Note how her "voice" in this essay makes her a more convincing writer.

form of liquid violence and conflict. Each of our addictions to

oil causes an individual, internal tension. Deep down many of

us know that we consume too much, that we're destroying

the earth, and that every gallon of gasoline we buy

contributes to the violence. What we fear is not just gas

station crime, but our own dependence and shame, our own

rationalizations and greed. And yet, like an addict pushing a

syringe, we keep pumping. Then we charge it to our plastic.

> Jennifer focuses on the bigger picture and the "so what?" in her conclusion (Chapter 7).

Works Cited

"Gas Station Theft Prevention." *National Crime Prevention*

   Council, 2008. Web. 30 March 2008.

"Gasoline Myths... and Facts." *The Association for*

   Convenience & Petroleum Retailing, 2008. Web. 31

   March 2008.

Hanania, Ray. "Fighting for the last victims of September 11."

   Hanania, n.d. Web. 31 March 2008.

"Identity Theft Statistics." *Spam Laws*, n.d. Web. 1 April 2008.

Kirk, Jeremy. "Gas Stations Ripe for ID Theft?" *PCWorld*, 26

   June, 2007. Web. 31 March 2008.

Margonelli, Lisa. *Oil on the Brain.* New York: DoubleDay, 2007.

   Print.

"Robbery: Crime in the United States." *The FBI, Federal*

   Bureau of Investigations, 2004. Web. 29 March, 2004.

Sample Essay Project 3

Quitting Cold Turkey
By Lydia Davidson

"Peter, we're having Tofurky for Thanksgiving this year," my father, Mark, said into the phone. There was a stunned pause on the other end of the line.

"No. Way," Peter, my twenty-six year old brother, finally responded.

My father relayed this conversation to me a few days before I flew home to Denver, Colorado for the much-anticipated Thanksgiving break. I had just completed my first nine weeks of college at Santa Clara University. We both laughed. Fun-loving and light-hearted, Peter had actually believed for a moment that our family was switching from the traditional Thanksgiving turkey to a tofu substitute. He had just posted his excitement about what he called "Turkey Day" on Facebook the day before. In his mind, not having a turkey for Thanksgiving was simply not a viable option.

My father cleared up the situation and explained to Peter that I had decided to become a vegetarian. Since I was just starting to switch to that food pattern though, I would

> **Trifecta:**
> Opening Paragraphs (Chapter 4).
>
> Lydia uses dialogue and personal narrative to engage the readers and help them identify with her and her family.

still be participating in Thanksgiving as usual. I would not be requesting any special menus yet. Don't worry. No Tofurky this year. After all, it is Thanksgiving we are talking about. The food is of the utmost importance.

Although the food is plentiful and delicious, it is not really what Thanksgiving is about in the Davidson household. We have a tradition of saying a special Thanksgiving prayer before the big feast to thank God for all of the blessings in our lives. Like many Americans, we spent this Thanksgiving together, just immediate family, cooking, eating, watching football, and playing cards. We laughed, joked, talked, and enjoyed each other's company. When I asked what Thanksgiving meant to each of my family members at dinner, they all came up with similar answers. These answers made it clear to me that, in our family, Thanksgiving is about love, fellowship, friendship, and our profound gratitude for the people and experiences in our lives. We all expressed love and thanks for each other, and for family members no longer able to join us at our table. We shared gratitude for the strong set of family values and deep bonds that we have with one another. We agreed that Thanksgiving means more than

> **Trifecta:** Opposition Paragraph (Chapter 4).

turkey and stuffing. It's a time to be together and reflect on what and whom we are grateful for. Our Thanksgiving is always filled with laughter, good conversation, and warmth.

But when I asked my family what they thought Thanksgiving meant to most Americans, I got very different answers.

"Black Friday," my mother piped in automatically, frowning.

"Consumerism," Peter mentioned, most likely remembering that his girlfriend could not join us because she had to waitress and serve people eating their Thanksgiving dinner at a restaurant.

Lydia is transitioning here from her opposition into her *Slant*, using dialogue and personal narrative to illuminate the controversy.

"An excuse to eat a ton of food," my father stated, gesturing to our packed plates.

The elephant in the room then became clear. Why on earth were we as a family participating in the American Thanksgiving rituals if they mean something so vastly different from our own definitions of Thanksgiving? Why are we eating one of the forty-six million turkeys eaten on Thanksgiving Day in the U.S. (Lyles)? Why are we watching the Macy's Thanksgiving Day Parade? I had to ask. The answer I got was unanimous and unsettling.

"Because we like it."

This is the underlying problem in my family's Thanksgiving. Yes, we do have values. We value family, friendship, love, honesty, and compassion to name a few. However, these values seem to contradict what we actually end up supporting on Thanksgiving. Worse than that, we *know* that there is a problem with the food we are eating and how Thanksgiving is celebrated through the unabashed buying and selling of everything possible. If we did not know, maybe we would have an excuse. But we do. We know it. And it makes us complicit in the corruption. We are failing to take responsibility for the fact that we are participating in Thanksgiving in a way that supports cruelty, consumerism, and corporate greed, all of which directly oppose our explicit values.

My family and I participate in Thanksgiving not because it reflects what we believe and value but because it gives pleasure and satisfies our simplest, most basic desires. We know that the Macy's Thanksgiving Day Parade (both

> **Trifecta:** Thesis Paragraph (Chapter 4).
>
> Notice how explicitly and strongly Lydia states her *Slant* in this paragraph, varying her sentence lengths to give the paragraph dynamism and impact.

while it is airing and in the commercial breaks) promotes the most obvious and despicable aspects of consumerism.

We know that the food labels of organic, natural, and free range that assuage our consciences are mostly meaningless and that the turkey on our dining room table came from a factory farm where it could not "walk normally, much less jump or fly" (Foer 111) and could never reproduce during its short and miserable life because "the suffering is in [its] genes" (113). In fact, according to Jonathan Safran Foer, author of national bestseller *Eating Animals*, "what we do to living turkeys is just about as bad as anything humans have ever done to any animal in the history of the world" (249).

We know that people will be working at stores

> Introducing sources using synthesis (Chapter 5).

> Lydia repeats the phrase "We know" as a transition and to give her paragraphs flow (Chapter 5).

starting on Thanksgiving for Black Friday sales. According to a poll done by *Allstate* and *National Journal*, a quarter of adult Americans work on Thanksgiving, Christmas or New Year's (Malcolm) and the majority of consumers are uncomfortable with stores opening on Thanksgiving (Clark), my family included. We look down on all of those traditions and practices. We agree that they are unsavory and unethical.

Yet here we are, Thanksgiving day, choosing to participate in all of these contradictions simply *because we like it.*

Our Thanksgiving could be made into a documentary called "American Thanksgiving." When I woke up I watched the Macy's Thanksgiving Day Parade and on commercial breaks helped my mother in the kitchen. Conscious of their health and showing great discipline, my father and Peter woke up early to work out at the gym, coming home later to help get everything ready for dinner. After the parade was over, we switched the channel to watch the Detroit Lions destroy the Philadelphia Eagles in football while we cooked the day's treats. First came hors d'oeuvres: honey smoked salmon on crackers, chips and clam dip, cheese, crab meat and crackers, and a veggie platter. Of course all of that paled in comparison to the main course: turkey, two types of stuffing, cranberry sauce, garlic mashed potatoes, mushroom soup, green beans, sweet potatoes, and carrots. We had to take a break to relax (and nap, in my case) before digging into the pumpkin and pecan pies. It isn't every day that we eat our weight in rich foods, but holidays are special occasions, and feasting is a way of celebrating. Food is one of the greatest

While Lydia's *Slant* focuses on her family, she is also sure to convey how her family is much like many American families. This encourages the reader to identify.

parts of any celebration. Yet why is it that something inherently good—coming together with others to celebrate life—is lived out in such an unhealthy manner? Needless to say, this holiday wasn't quite the "no-guilt Thanksgiving" of portion controlled plates suggested on the internet (Sass).

> Lydia repeats the phrase "portion control" as a transition (Chapter 5).

Of course, it shouldn't be said that portion control could possibly alleviate guilt after the materialism built around Thanksgiving. The Macy's Thanksgiving Day Parade, which started out in 1924 as a way to draw attention to the New York City Macy's store, has grown immensely. It now brings over 3.5 million people to New York City each year in addition to the fifty million television viewers (Macy's). While it started as just a way to sell Macy's, it now promotes tourism, celebrities, fishing/hunting, cartoons, movies, television shows, stores, food, and even ways of life. It is consumerist heaven. Yet we still sit around the television for four hours and watch floats and balloons representing everything we buy into pass by. While watching the parade, my mother and I discussed how sad it is that Thanksgiving has come to be a holiday of materialism. But did we turn off the television?

The parade pairs well with another event that has unfortunately leached into Thanksgiving: Black Friday. Black Friday, always the day after Thanksgiving, is the largest shopping day of the year in the United States. With huge sales and deals, customers flood the stores. In 2014, consumers spent $50,900,000,000 in stores and another $1,505,000,000 online, coming out at an average of $380.95 per person ("Black Friday"). From 2006-2014, Black Friday was directly responsible for seven deaths and ninety-eight injuries, ranging from shootings to being trampled by the hordes of shoppers ("Black Friday Death Count"). Not only are people spending inordinate amounts of time and money on one day of shopping, but some consumers become so invested in their shopping that they harm others and/or themselves. Many of the commercials during Thanksgiving football games and television programs even boast what is now dubbed "Black Thursday" (Edelson). Thanksgiving, it seems, is not a time for family, but a time to shop. Even a family-oriented holiday is a chance to profit off of early holiday shoppers. Why not entice people to abandon their families to get that early deal on Thanksgiving? Every dollar

> Lydia uses her research to examine and support the contradiction between values and behavior in her own family.
>
> Notice how she pairs her research with her family's Thanksgiving throughout the essay.

counts. Black Friday sales now open as early as 3:00 pm on Thanksgiving Day.

My brother is all too familiar with heading into work for a 5:00 p.m. - 3:00 a.m. shift on Thanksgiving, as he has had to work multiple Thanksgivings, leaving early from dinner to make it in time. As we watched football on Thanksgiving, we commiserated, saying how horrible it was that people had to work retail jobs on what should be a family holiday. We aren't the only ones who are upset either. Since Black Friday has increasingly encroached on Thanksgiving, people have held strikes and protests against corporations—most notably, what have become annual protests by Wal-Mart workers in multiple states who have become a "rallying cry" against Wal-Mart and other corporations that open on Thanksgiving day (Jamieson). But the fact is that instant gratification has become the name of the game. The more the better and the sooner the better.

My family really did not have much of a right to complain though; we have had many Thanksgiving trips to the grocery store to pick up last-minute supplies. In fact, we often take that for granted—that others are working while we feast. With the massive amounts of food consumed on Thanksgiving, these feasts come with massive costs. The turkey is the food that most calls into question the meaning of Thanksgiving. To start, it is unlikely that turkey was eaten at all at the first Thanksgiving in 1621 (Reed). Even if turkey was on the menu, the factory farmed turkeys that we feast on bear little to no resemblance to turkeys of the 17th Century. I brought this up to my family on Thanksgiving by asking a follow up question.

> Lydia continues to use dialogue in the essay—a stylistic choice she made in the opening paragraphs.
>
> The dialogue gives her essay personality, life, and humor.

"How similar do you think our turkey is to a wild turkey?"

"Lydia, what are you even talking about?" Peter asked.

"Or a heritage turkey with the plumage and feathers? How similar do you think they are, or would be if they were both alive?"

"Ours would be bloated? Could barely walk, right?" my mother asked.

I nodded. "And it was all a product of artificial insemination. Factory farmed turkeys can't even reproduce. This turkey could not be found in nature" (Foer 111).

"Well, Lydia, you bring up an interesting point. Seconds anyone?" my father said, trying to ease the palpable tension.

My family did not want to talk about what they were eating. My parents listened to my rants over the phone while I was at school, but when I brought up an uncomfortable issue at the scene of the crime, there was less open accommodation. Peter, on his second or third helping, certainly did not want what he was eating to be called into question. My family did not want to admit that the turkey we consumed was a waddling, hormone-ridden, product of artificial insemination and misery. They certainly did not want to hear that industrial turkey farms "have incinerators to burn all of the turkeys that die every day" because "sick animals are more profitable" and quantity beats quality (Foer 111).

Lydia pairs her family narrative with research to persuade the reader.

There is just something too good about eating turkey, about turkey being the centerpiece of a food-filled holiday. I was disrupting the atmosphere by criticizing the food on our table, taking away from the meaning of Thanksgiving and the privilege of excess.

But maybe Thanksgiving does not actually mean family values to us. Maybe our actions speak louder than our words.

I managed to not totally ruin Thanksgiving for my family. I was worried that bringing up controversy and the complete paradox that Thanksgiving entails would destroy the positive vibe of a family Thanksgiving, and maybe even infect our relationships. It was quite uncomfortable to bring up the issues that I have with Thanksgiving. I did not want to ruin our family holiday. After all, I was only home for a week, and quality time with my family is precious. It turns out that I didn't need to be worried. After my prodding and questioning, everything went back to normal. My pointed comments and sarcastic quips were equated with my newfound college independence, not as legitimate claims and challenges.

What I was saying challenged the norm that is American Thanksgiving. It is not just about what we are doing, but what we think and feel about what we are doing. As pinpointed by Dr. Allan G. Johnson, an author, speaker, and professor of sociology, in his book *The Forest and the*

Lydia begins to transition into another important point here that will end with her essay's conclusion. Her observation about her family's failure to take her seriously will connect with a larger problem she sees in many Americans' actions when it comes to injustices.

Trees: Sociology as Life, Practice, and Promise, normal is based not on actions but ideas about actions (Johnson 44) and Thanksgiving is a crown jewel of all that is seen as righteous and good in America. While we ignore and push away the fact that our actions are unacceptable, we allow ourselves to deny our responsibility, creating a Thanksgiving mythology that rationalizes all the wretchedness. It takes courage and will to strip away the layers of falsity and pretense wrapped around habits, customs and norms and see them for what they are, especially when it comes to something as universal as food. Are we really prepared to look critically at ourselves and change our ways when we aren't happy with what we find? Can we look at our food without the pomp and circumstance, or must we accept that food is not rational but is "culture, habit, and identity" (Foer 263)?

Perhaps both are possible. Culture is fluid; we constantly make and remake the world around us. Maybe when I go home for Christmas break I'll refuse to eat the meat-filled Italian food that is on our dinner table. Maybe next year my family will eat succotash instead of turkey. However, the truth is that possibility is not probability, and it is much easier to turn our heads and stick to the status quo. We are socialized to stick to the norms. When we deviate, we often face questions, skepticism, eye-rolls, and sometimes even disdain. Try telling your family you'd rather not participate in the genocide of cruelly-treated, corporate, factory-farmed turkeys on Thanksgiving and see if you get acceptance, agreement, and a pat on the back. No, denial and complicity are the options that offer the least amount of backlash.

> That idea of complicity that Lydia developed in her Crescendo Analysis resurfaces here in her concluding paragraphs.

Thanksgiving is certainly not the only place where social norms create difficult moral dilemmas. Injustice is everywhere. It permeates our families, communities, and the world. So many of us turn a blind eye. Yet, there are some who fight for justice, who change their minds, hearts and actions to fight those things that oppose their values. It's always easier to say, "Someone else will fight this" or "My contribution cannot possibly make a difference," but that is exactly the type of thinking that allows for injustice and blocks positive change. Each choice to change has a ripple effect. It is crucial, and, yes, it is difficult. It is a heavy burden to put into action the part of your heart that wants to "save

the world." But if not my family and me, then who?

Lydia focuses on the bigger picture and the "so what?" in her conclusion, but also implicates the reader by challenging herself and her own family in this last sentence (Chapter 7).

Any idea why Lydia decided to break a grammatical rule here and use "who" instead of "whom" in the last sentence?

HINT: What rhymes with "who"?

Works Cited

"Black Friday Consumer Spending Statistics." *Statistic Brain*. Statistic

Brain Research Institute, n.d. Web. 7 May 2016.

"Black Friday Death Count." *Black Friday Death Count*.

Blackfridaydeathcount.com, n.d. Web. 29 April 2016.

Clark, Kelsey. "Working on Thanksgiving Day? Here's Why Most

People Don't Want You Too." *Deseret News National*. Deseret

Digital Media, 25 Nov. 2014. Web. 8 May 2016.

Edelson, Sharon. "Thanksgiving Backlash." *Women's Wear Daily*, 14

Nov. 2012. Web. 17 Nov. 2015.

Foer, Jonathan Safran. *Eating Animals*. New York: Little, Brown, 2009.

Print.

Jameson, Dave. "Walmart Workers Launch Black Friday Strike."

Huffpost Business. TheHuffingtonPost.com, Inc., 26 Nov. 2014.

Web. 8 May 2016.

Johnson, Allan G. *The Forest and the Trees: Sociology as Life, Practice, and Promise*. Third ed. Philadelphia: Temple UP, 2014. Print.

Lyles, Toby, and Amy Roberts. "Thanksgiving by the Numbers." *CNN*. Cable News Network, 25 Nov. 2014. Web. 17 Nov. 2015.

"Macy's Thanksgiving Day Parade History." *Macy's Thanksgiving Day Parade History*. NYCTourist, 1996-2015. Web. 29 Nov. 2015.

Malcolm, Hadley. "Quarter of Americans Will Work over Holidays." *USA Today*, 25 Nov. 2014. Web. 5 May 2016.

Reed, Julia. "Fowl Ball." *Newsweek* 23 Nov. 2009: 63. *Biography in Context*. Web. 17 Nov. 2015.

Sass, Cynthia. "Happy No-Guilt Thanksgiving!" *Health*, Nov. 2013: 57. Print.

The *Slant* Essay Rubric
(Download rubric at www.NicholasLeither.com)

A Exemplary The essay contains a clear and appropriately-specific thesis/*Slant* that suggests original and independent thinking. The body offers detailed and meaningful support for the argument, and uses that support logically and insightfully; it offers progressive and unified paragraphs, and clearly connects the support with the thesis/*Slant*. The conclusion provokes the reader, leaving him/her with a question or idea about the bigger implications of the essay's thesis/*Slant*. The essay contains clear logic, appropriate grammar, and correct spelling. The language, tone and argument are appropriately tailored to its intended audience; the writing and ideas are dynamic, varied and creative.	Comments:
B Accomplished The essay contains a clear and appropriately-specific thesis/*Slant*. The body offers sufficient and detailed support for the argument, displays unified paragraphs, and connects support with the thesis/*Slant*. The conclusion brings the essay to a satisfactory close. The essay contains clear logic, appropriate grammar, and correct spelling. Its language and argument are appropriate for the intended audience, and fluent throughout the essay.	Comments:
C Satisfactory The essay contains a thesis/*Slant*, but that thesis/*Slant* may need specificity and/or clarity. The body offers adequate support for the argument, but the paragraphs may contain too little support or too much opinion, and may fail to fully connect supporting points to the core thesis/*Slant*. The conclusion may be repetitive or fail to offer bigger insights. The essay contains few errors in logic, grammar, and spelling. Its language and argument may at times be flawed, awkward, and repetitive.	Comments:
D Limited The essay does not contain a clear and/or specific thesis/*Slant*. The body may offer inadequate support, display an incomplete grasp of the topic, or use support illogically. Because the essay has a flawed argument and structure, the conclusion may either fail to provoke the reader or offer closure. The essay contains errors in logic, grammar, and spelling. Its language and argument are inadequate.	Comments:
F Failure This essay either fails to fulfill the assignment or does not contain an argument or *Slant*, support for an argument, citation, or readable language.	Comments:

SLANT

WWW.NICHOLASLEITHER.COM

Made in the USA
San Bernardino, CA
08 July 2017